PROVIDED BY:

Beth Burkeen, CPA
BURKEENandASSOCIATES

www.burkeenandassociates.com

ULTIMATE
PRODUCTIVITY

A CUSTOMIZED GUIDE TO DISCOVERING YOUR PERSONAL PATH TO SUCCESS

BY JIM STOVALL
FOREWORD BY STEVE FORBES

THOMAS NELSON
Since 1798

NASHVILLE   DALLAS   MEXICO CITY   RIO DE JANEIRO   BEIJING

Published in Nashville, Tennessee, by Thomas Nelson. Thomas Nelson is a registered trademark of Thomas Nelson, Inc.

Thomas Nelson, Inc. books may be purchased in bulk for educational, business, fund-raising, or sales promotional use. For information, please e-mail SpecialMarkets@ThomasNelson.com.

Library of Congress Cataloging-in-Publication Data

Stovall, Jim.
  Ultimate productivity : a customized guide to discovering your personal path to success / by Jim Stovall ; foreword by Steve Forbes.
    p. cm.
  ISBN 978-0-7852-2888-2 (hardcover)
  1. Success in business. 2. Success. 3. Motivation (Psychology) 4. Employee motivation. I. Title.
  HF5386.S8827 2008
  658.4'09—dc22

2008005164

Printed in the United States of America
08 09 10 11 12 QW 8 7 6 5 4 3 2 1

DEDICATION

This book is dedicated to Dorothy Thompson whose hard work turns my words into books and to Rebeka Graham whose collaboration has made *Ultimate Productivity* more than just a book.

CONTENTS

Acknowledgments vii

Foreword by Steve Forbes ix

Chapter One: The Beginning: Start Where You Are 1

Chapter Two: Success: Forging Your Own Definition 11

Chapter Three: Mission: Your Journey Toward Success 21

Chapter Four: Productivity: A Powerful Measure of Life 31

Chapter Five: Customizing: Fulfilling Your Unique Potential 41

Chapter Six: Passion: The Cause and Effect 49

Chapter Seven: Discovery: Three Powerful Tools 61

Chapter Eight: Honest Assessment: Getting into Position 71

Chapter Nine: Motivation: A Magic Machine 83

Chapter Ten: Establishing Motivational Miracles 95

Chapter Eleven: The Communication Contradiction 107

Chapter Twelve: Communications: Customizing Your Message . . 121

Chapter Thirteen: The Implementation Enigma 133

Chapter Fourteen: Implementation: Pulling the Trigger 145

Chapter Fifteen: Action: Now or Never 159

About the Author. 165

ACKNOWLEDGMENTS

I would like to acknowledge Steve Forbes for his leadership, friendship, and willingness to be a part of *Ultimate Productivity*. I would like to acknowledge Coach Wooden for sharing his legendary experience and wisdom with all of us through this book. I would like to thank Dr. Denis Waitley and Ken Blanchard for their support and encouragement of *Ultimate Productivity*. I would like to acknowledge our entire team at the Narrative Television Network for their efforts to bring my message to the world, and I would like to thank everyone at Thomas Nelson for stepping out and being willing to publish my first book over a decade ago and now being willing to reconnect on this breakthrough project.

FOREWORD
BY STEVE FORBES

I became aware of Jim Stovall in the late '90s, when we at Forbes were compiling a book that was subsequently released in 2000, entitled *Forbes Great Success Stories: Twelve Tales of Victory Wrested from Defeat*. That book contained Jim Stovall's story along with those of Donald Trump, Tom Monaghan, and others whose real-life adventures in capitalism point out what makes our system the best in the world.

I was then proud to endorse Jim's book *The Ultimate Gift*, which, at this writing, has sold 4 million copies around the world and has been made into a major motion picture from Twentieth Century Fox starring James Garner, Brian Dennehy, and Abigail Breslin.

I have been quoted as calling Jim Stovall one of the greatest men of our era—not solely for the things he has done, but for the fact that Jim Stovall has dissected his own success and put it on display for others to follow through his speeches, newspaper columns, and books such as the one you hold now.

In *Ultimate Productivity*, Jim Stovall strikes at the heart of success and failure for all of us individually and as a society. Natural and human resources abound, but how we harness them to create our own personal success is determined by our ingenuity and productivity. In this book, you will learn how to maximize your own productivity by discovering and releasing your core strengths in the critical areas of motivation, communication, and implementation.

I believe if we will let Jim Stovall lead us through our own Ultimate Productivity Profile, we will all become better people and grow closer to our potential. In the final analysis, we cannot be judged in comparison to anyone or anything but only in the reflection of our individualized mirror that reveals our potential.

CHAPTER ONE

THE BEGINNING:
START WHERE YOU ARE

I am grateful to you and everyone who takes the time and makes the effort to buy and read one of my books. By virtue of the fact that you selected this book, I assume that there are aspects of your life that you would like to change, develop, or improve. If this is the case, read on. If this is not the case, and you are truly satisfied with every area of your personal and professional life, stop reading this book immediately and go get a refund.

This may be the third book you have read this month. On the other hand, it might be the first book you've read since high school. I have had an interesting relationship with books throughout my life. For the first half of my life, I don't know that I ever read an entire book cover to cover. I got through high school, and even college, reading as little as necessary to matriculate through the process.

This seems ironic to me today, because when I had my eyesight and could read the words on a page as you are doing now, I never did it. Then, at age 29, I began my life as a totally blind person and, from that day to this thanks to books on tape from the Library for the Blind and a high speed tape recorder, I have actually read a book every day.

Having spent the last twenty years completing a full-length book each day, I have formed a unique relationship with books. They have become a major part of my life. I have read thousands of books for both entertainment and information. But I have also read a handful of books for transformation. These books have impacted me so deeply that they have changed who I am and how I live my life. My fervent hope is that this book will bring that kind of transformational experience to you.

Within these pages, you will have the opportunity to define your own success, create a life mission to achieve success, forge productivity on your own terms, and then begin to succeed by effectively utilizing motivation, communication, and implementation.

As an author, columnist, and speaker in the field of personal development, I have been exposed to many success systems, theories, and philosophies. They all have a certain degree of validity. But I feel, in many ways, the current state-of-the-art in the field of success and achievement is lacking a critical component.

There are many books or systems that will teach you to set a goal, create milestones, pursue your passion, and make changes in your world. These are important steps, but unless you have the practical tools to achieve and succeed at your fingertips, you don't have a chance.

> Only by accepting full responsibility for your *past*, which has resulted in your *present*, can you then take control of your actions *today* and create a successful tomorrow.

Let's assume that I wanted to be a champion golfer. Even if this *goal* was firmly established in my mind, and I pursued it with passion and exhibited the highest degree of determination, I would be doomed to failure without practical, realistic instruction. And even if I did seek advice from the best golfer in the world—even Tiger Woods himself—I still wouldn't have a chance unless his instructions were mechanically sound for and specific to *me*.

If Tiger Woods simply told me to hit the ball farther than anyone else, straight down the fairway, and never forget to make every putt inside of twenty feet—but then he left me to my own devices, my game would never improve, and my goal of being a champion golfer would go to my grave with me, as most people's goals and passions do with them. But if my instruction included mastering motivation, communication, and implementation, as you are going to discover it through Ultimate Productivity, I would have the opportunity to succeed as a golfer.

Before you learn to master and apply these principles, it is vital for you to decide what changes you want to bring into your life. In order to make this kind of decision, you first need to establish where you are today and take full responsibility for your current state—in every area of your life. Only by accepting full responsibility for your past, which has resulted in your current condition, can you then take control of your actions today and create a successful tomorrow.

We live in a society full of people who love to blame their mediocrity on everyone and everything other than themselves. As a corporate and arena speaker, I have had the privilege of talking with literally millions of people. After some of these events, I often visit with members of my audience. Oftentimes, these people share with me that their lives are not where they want them to be. They are not pursuing their passions, nor reaching their goals. But they invariably hasten to add, "If you knew my family, you would know why I'm not succeeding." Or, "I'm where I am today because my boss is an idiot, and the weather's too hot, and the taxes are too high . . . and besides that, Jim, I'm a middle child."

When it comes to failure, one excuse is about as good as another. In fact, the next time your life is not turning out the way you want it to, don't blame anyone else, just use my world-famous Jim Stovall, one-size-fits-all, 100% money-back-guaranteed excuse for all situations. Here is how it works. Instead of blaming anyone or anything around you for your condition, simply locate the nearest mirror, look directly into it, and say these magic words: "I guess I really didn't want it that bad." This will work for you every time because unless or until you accept responsibility for the choices you have made in the past that have brought you to this place, you can never take control of your future.

The most destructive lies we ever tell are those we tell ourselves.

Now, I can hear you thinking that I don't understand your situation, your background, and the barriers you face. That's true, and I certainly realize that bad things can happen to good people. But for every person you can show me who has been defeated by a given circumstance, I can show you others who have faced that same circumstance and have used it as a springboard to do greater and more significant things in their lives.

But before you determine where you want to go in the world, there is one critical navigational element. You must first establish exactly where you are. Maps, directions, and even global positioning devices can only help you reach your destination if your current position is established.

For example, if you want to be wealthy, then before you decide what "wealthy" means to you, you'd better establish your present financial position. If you want to lose weight, you've got to get on the scales today. To create the lifestyle of your dreams, in every area of your personal and professional existence, you've got to be totally honest with yourself and elicit the honest opinions of those around you.

This honest assessment is a difficult process, because we have a tendency to judge everyone else's performance while judging our own intentions. It's easy for us to smugly assert, without reservation, that the other guy was inexcusably late for his appointment. But when we find ourselves running behind schedule, it was simply that we missed every traffic light; we had to stop for gas; and who knew that there would be a traffic jam, a detour, and road construction en route to our destination?

If you're going to live the life of your dreams through Ultimate Productivity by mastering motivation, communication, and implementation, you're going to have to be totally honest with yourself about where you are. The most destructive lies we ever tell are those we tell ourselves, because after a while we start to believe these falsehoods and begin sharing them with the world as if they were true.

> A person who doesn't *make* a choice is no better off than a person who doesn't *have* a choice.

A convincing character played by one of my favorite actors, Jack Nicholson, in one of his best movies, uttered these famous words: "You can't handle the truth." While it's not easy and never fun, I want you to know that you can handle the truth, and it will be your first step toward making your life everything you want it to be.

As you accept responsibility for where you are and the choices you have made, you will begin to discover that while you have made some bad choices, in many cases you are mired in mediocrity because you have made no choice at all.

I believe that in this world there are a few people who make good choices, and they enjoy every reward they seek. There are a few people who make bad choices, and they live in places like Leavenworth and San Quentin. But then there are the vast majority of people who make neither good nor bad choices, but, instead, they make no choice at all. These are the people who neither make things happen nor watch things happen. They simply don't realize that anything happened.

I am reminded of a story about Irish immigrants coming to the United States during the earliest part of the twentieth century. One particular family saved for many years to get passage for the mother, father, and three children. Yet even with all of their diligent effort, they were only able to save enough to purchase a ticket in what was known as "steerage": a small, cramped area below deck, where they had to both sleep and pass the many days of the transatlantic voyage.

The family had brought some bread, cheese, and water to sustain them through the journey, but they rapidly consumed all of their rations with many days left in the voyage. From their squalid quarters below deck, they could see through the cracks between the planking onto the main deck above them. They could observe first-class passengers dressed in all of their finery, devouring a sumptuous banquet just a few feet away from where they were literally starving.

Finally, in desperation, the father crawled down the passageway, stepped up onto the main deck, and asked one of the stewards if he could have a few scraps or leftovers, lest his family starve to death below deck. The shocked steward replied, "Sir, this banquet is provided three times daily for all of our passengers. You and your family have been starving when you could have been feasting on the very best all along."

Before you launch into your quest to make your life everything you want it to be through Ultimate Productivity, be sure you have set your sights high enough. A person who doesn't make a choice is no better off than a person who doesn't have a choice at all; but a person who accepts less than their true destiny is relegated to a life of mediocrity. When you have seen yourself in your mind's eye on top of the world, anything less will leave you wanting.

We have all had dreams and secret passions inside of us for many years. When we were teenagers or young adults, the world seemed pregnant with possibility. But somewhere between there and here, this thing we call reality set in, and we got so busy making a living that we forgot to create a life.

Your destiny awaits.

NOTES:

CHAPTER TWO

SUCCESS:
FORGING YOUR OWN DEFINITION

Whether you're reading my book or anyone else's that purports to guide you to success, you first need to agree on a definition of success—and be sure the person leading you knows how to get there.

All of my grandparents and both of my parents come from a pleasant town called Springfield. My brother Bob and his family live there to this day. Springfield has much to recommend it in the way of historical sites and recreational activities.

Let's say you and I agree to meet for a long weekend in Springfield to discuss our respective professional and personal goals, as well as to enjoy some of the local attractions. This sounds like a pleasant prospect to me, as I hope it would to you. But unless you were acquainted with my family, you and I would have a tremendous challenge getting together, because there are more than thirty U.S. cities and towns named Springfield.

I'm sure many of the various Springfields have wonderful attractions and notable attributes; however, unless we agree on the same Springfield, we will not get together, and my directions and roadmaps will be useless to you.

In each of the thirty-plus Springfields across the country, there are both people who were born and raised there, and those who have chosen "Springfield" as the best place for them and their families to live their lives. Millions of people call Springfield home, but they do not all mean the same thing when they use the words *Springfield* and *home*.

Success is much the same. I am convinced that there are as many definitions for *success* as there are people. More people fail, not because they are unable to reach their goals, but because they have wrongly defined both their goals and the meaning of *success*.

> More people fail, not because they are unable to reach their goals, but because they have wrongly defined both their goals and the meaning of *success*.

The meaning of *success* is probably the most private and personal definition you will ever establish; therefore, as you work toward creating your own picture of success, you can accept only limited help along the way. As if this weren't difficult enough, the challenge is compounded when you realize that your definition of success will be constantly changing throughout your life.

> You can become the greatest financial success the world has ever known, but if you lose your family and ruin your health in the process, you will not be successful.

Many self-proclaimed success gurus encourage us to compartmentalize our success. They may label these compartments *financial* success, *business* success, *family* success, *fitness* success, etc. While I would agree that these are all components of personal success, you can't truly *succeed* while doing well in one area but failing miserably in another.

The *Titanic*, which had been called "unsinkable" as it was being built and launched, became the most famous ship of all time for doing the one thing no one wants a ship to do: sink. There may be many definitions of a successful ship—

whether it be militarily, financially, aesthetically, or in over-all performance—but I think we can all agree that, in ship terms, *sinking* could be synonymous with *failure*.

When the *Titanic* was constructed, it was built with a number of watertight compartments. The engineers designed the *Titanic* to stay afloat even if several of these compart-ments were flooded. Unfortunately, all of the compartments were connected at the top, so when the *Titanic* hit an iceberg in the North Atlantic, the water that flooded several of the compartments overflowed at the top and flooded the entire ship; therefore, the *Titanic* sank.

Success is much the same way. Failure in any area will affect all areas.

Think of success as a three-legged stool. For the sake of this analogy, you might have a financial-success leg, a family-success leg, and a physical-success leg. You can become the greatest financial success the world has ever known, but if you lose your family and ruin your health in the process, you will not be successful, even if the whole world views you as a success.

Our media-driven society has created a phenomenon over the past several decades that is unique to our modern culture. Through magazines, television, radio, the Internet, and every other means of communication, we are bombarded with information about people and how they live. People have become famous in ways they never were before. We have always admired famous athletes, artists, and actors, but now we can learn where they spend their vacations, what they like to eat for breakfast, and the name of their dog. We know every sordid detail of not only their professional lives, but also their personal lives. We constantly consume information and images about the lifestyles of the rich and famous and how some people are rising to the pinnacle of our society while others are falling from that same pinnacle and plummeting toward the depths of disgrace.

> In my life, I have been very poor and very rich. All other things being equal, rich is better.

In this environment, it is easy to get a warped view of success. One of the big lies we are bombarded regularly with, is the corrupting thought that if we had enough money, all our problems would be solved. Yet one need look no farther than the daily headlines to learn how some of the wealthiest among us have lost their health, sacrificed their families, disregarded their integrity, and subjected themselves to all manner of human failure.

Recent studies of people around the world, from the wealthiest to those living in abject poverty, reveal that beyond the basic necessities of food, clothing, and shelter, more money doesn't make us happy and, therefore, successful.

Any discussion of money and success would be lacking if I did not state that money is neither good nor bad. In the hands of good people, money can build places of healing, worship, and learning. In the hands of bad people, money can create destruction, disease, and death. In my life, I have been very poor and very rich. All other things being equal, never forget that rich is better.

While money, in and of itself, will not create success, I believe from my personal and professional contact that Bill Gates, Warren Buffett, and Steve Forbes are each, in their own way, quite successful. Yet they are not successful because they have amassed great wealth; they are successful because they have created value in the lives of other people. This created value has brought them wealth, and they have utilized their financial success to make the world a better place. If money were a prerequisite to being successful, we would all have to agree that Mother Teresa was an absolute failure.

Fame and notoriety have been mistakenly labeled as success by many in our society. People's names have become household words for playing baseball, being on a television show, eating insects on an island, or dating a famous person. There are even people today who are famous for nothing more than being famous. As a society, we have all gotten caught up in a massive parade, and no one has yet stopped to take a deep breath and consider the fact that we're not following these people because they're famous. They're famous because we're following them.

> Success comes when you live a life of productivity on a mission toward a worthwhile goal.

Fame, in and of itself, is not a factor in success. Some of the most famous people in the twentieth century include Winston Churchill, Franklin Roosevelt, Adolf Hitler, John F. Kennedy, Sandra Day O'Connor, Martin Luther King Jr., and Lee Harvey Oswald. Some of these lived lives of great success, while others were miserable failures in spite of their fame.

Some of the most successful people in the world will never be known by anyone other than those whose lives they powerfully and positively impact. These people have defined success in such a manner that achieving their life goals does not bring them fame and notoriety. In some cases, their anonymity is a by-product of their success goal, and in other cases they have defined success, at least partially, as living their lives away from the spotlight.

Success has, furthermore, been misdefined as being young, healthy, or beautiful. While these are all desirable traits in the right time and place, they are not a sole determinant of what we would call success. Those who worship at the altar of youth and beauty will necessarily find themselves fighting a losing battle. Your hairdresser, tailor, and plastic surgeon can only do so much. If you live long enough, defined totally by the image in the mirror, you will fail due to your own misguided definition of success.

While you will have to fill in the details, and the specific elements of your own success, when it's all said and done, you will find that success comes when you live a life of productivity on a mission toward a worthwhile goal that brings you happiness, passion, and fulfillment.

NOTES:

CHAPTER THREE

MISSION:
YOUR JOURNEY TOWARD SUCCESS

Every few years, a new hot topic emerges among business writers, speakers, and consultants. These people are constantly on a quest to reinvent the wheel or, at least, new books, speeches, and consulting contracts. The same things that made people successful in the nineteenth century will bring you success in the twenty-first century.

Success is simple, but the mission toward success is never easy if you have established a worthwhile, significant, and meaningful goal. If you are a mountain climber, your goal might be to climb Mount Everest. If this is the case, you have now established a goal and defined success in your own terms. This is the simple part. Your mission is what you will find to be the not-so-easy part.

With tremendous preparation, sacrifice, and effort, you're going to have to start at the bottom of Mount Everest and make your way to the top; therefore, success is a destination even if it's a moving target, while your mission is that ongoing, constant journey toward success.

Several years ago in corporate America, it became trendy for each organization to establish a "mission statement." I don't mean to diminish the validity of creating and maintaining a corporate mission statement. Very few organizations have a mission statement that is really valid and meaningful to the people tasked with creating success. Unless their corporate mission statement is carved in granite on the outside of their building or suspended in gold leaf in the reception area, most employees don't even know there is a mission statement, much less what it might be.

There is a fundamental disconnect between most organizations and their established mission statements. If you came into an organization as a cold outside observer and simply watched the collective activity day after day, it would be difficult to discern their mission statement.

The engraved platitude memorialized in stone outside corporate headquarters may say, "We exist to provide the best products and services for each and every one of our customers and, in doing so, we endeavor to improve their lives and create peace on earth and goodwill toward men."

But if you observe the average employee, you might surmise that same corporation's mission statement to be, "We come to work as late as we can, do as little as possible, and avoid interaction with executives and customers so as to continue receiving a paycheck and benefits as long as humanly possible." Not only are such employees not pursuing their own goals; they have also found themselves on someone else's mission, for which they feel no passion, energy, or commitment. This does not make them bad people. It makes them misguided souls wandering through a world of limitless opportunity and possibility, in which they are not engaged.

As important as it may be for organizations to have a mission statement that is truly meaningful to all concerned, it is even more important that you and I each have a personal mission statement that defines our personal and professional journeys toward our own definitions of success.

I have had a personal mission statement of this kind for several years. I would like to tell you that I created it by myself, but in reality, my personal mission statement was given to me by my grandmother.

My grandmother played a vital role at several critical points in my life. When I was very young, my older sister became very ill with what was later diagnosed as a form of leukemia. Due to her illness and my parents' subsequent travels taking her from hospital to hospital and specialist to specialist across the country, I spent a lot of time with my grandparents. In fact, some of my earliest memories are of the valuable lessons I learned from them. They had lived through a depression, a world war, and the building of what we know as the modern world. They were part of what Tom Brokaw collectively labeled as the Greatest Generation. While I agree with Mr. Brokaw's assessment, I don't believe that their generation was created with any more greatness than we are. They were simply confronted with circumstances that required great people.

Success is a destination while your mission is that ongoing, constant journey toward success.

Several years later, as a teenager, I was diagnosed with a very serious eye disease that would eventually rob me of my sight. In that time of adjustment from being fully sighted to partially sighted and then moving into blindness, my grandmother was a tremendous support and encouragement. Through her words and deeds, she taught me the difference between *sight* and *vision*. I learned that sight is the ability to see the world around you by capturing images *through your eyes* and interpreting them in your mind. Vision is the ability to capture the world around you *in your mind*, as it should be, and make it a reality. Both sight and vision are valuable commodities, but as a person who has lived with and without both, given the choice, I would prefer vision to sight.

In my twenties, I spent some time as a Wall Street investment broker. Later, as a totally blind person, I launched a company called the Narrative Television Network, which makes movies, television, and educational programming accessible to 13 million blind and visually impaired Americans, and many millions more around the world. Through that process of building a successful company and being recognized first at the White House as the Entrepreneur of the Year and then by the U.S. Chamber of Commerce as the Businessperson of the Year, I began receiving invitations to speak at corporate and arena events across the country.

Somehow, as happens to all of us, years passed without my noticing, and my grandmother became quite elderly and was approaching the end of her life. Arrangements were made so she could spend most of her last months, weeks, and days in her own home, surrounded by the people and things she loved and that made her most comfortable. During this time, I made quite a few trips to see her.

On what turned out to be my last visit, I arrived after she was already asleep for the night. When her nurse, seated outside of her room, greeted me, I told her I wished I could have arrived earlier in the day, but a business commitment had delayed me. The nurse then told me that my grandmother was aware of that and was very proud of the work I did.

This really surprised me, as I had never known that my grandmother really understood what I did for a living. Sometimes when you're the first entrepreneur in your family, it's a little hard for the elder generations to grasp the concept.

Seeing my surprise, the nurse laughed softly, took my hand, and quietly led me through the doorway into my grandmother's room. Then she whispered, "Beside her bed there is a picture of you holding the Emmy award you received. Every person that comes into this house receives the same explanation from your grandmother. She points to that picture and tells them, 'This is my grandson. He does two things: He helps blind people see television, and he travels around the world, telling people they can have good things in their lives.'"

As impactful as that was at that time, the true import of it is still dawning on me, many years later. I didn't realize it then, and I'm quite certain my grandmother never heard of a personal mission statement, but through a private-duty night nurse, my grandmother had unknowingly given me my personal mission statement.

As I dictate these words, I am sitting in the office of my ever-growing business called the Narrative Television Network, and my most sincere desire is that these words are telling you that you *can* have good things in your life.

Anyone who has ever achieved a degree of what we would all call success has been on a mission. Their mission is clear, concise, and easily stated. John F. Kennedy set a goal in the '60s: America would put a man on the moon and bring him safely back to earth. That launched a mission for us all that culminated at the end of that same decade, when Neil Armstrong stepped on the surface of the moon and returned to earth safely. Had you asked Neil Armstrong during that time about his mission, I'm quite certain it would have been stated very clearly that he was, indeed, on his way to the moon.

During the darkest days of World War II, when Winston Churchill uttered some of the most profound statements ever voiced by a human being, he did more to win the war than anyone else. Churchill never fired a shot or captured an enemy soldier, but he won the war by defining our mission in terms that everyone understood. He articulated what our success would be and clarified that failure was intolerable.

Before you master productivity through motivation, communication, and implementation, it is vital that you define success and clarify your mission.

NOTES:

CHAPTER FOUR

PRODUCTIVITY:
A POWERFUL MEASURE OF LIFE

Productivity is probably one of the most misunderstood elements of success. The word *productive* is a derivative of the word *produce*, which, quite simply, means "to generate results." As we have already learned, in order to be successful, you have to make choices, define success in your own terms, and create a mission that will take you toward your ultimate destiny; therefore, as we look at Ultimate Productivity, it can only be gauged or measured in light of your personalized success goals.

Just because you're moving, it does not mean you're moving in the right direction. Visualize the hamster in the cage, frantically running on the spinning wheel. He has a lot of *activity* but no *productivity*. If the hamster runs even faster, he still doesn't get anywhere.

Be careful to never confuse activity with productivity. Most people in our society work very hard in terms of activity, and we all fill twenty-four hours each day and seven days each week; but, as in the case of our hamster friend, just because we're running or even sprinting doesn't mean we're really moving at all in terms of *productive progress* toward our personalized success goals.

It is actually astonishing to realize that, in some cases, activity can be counterproductive. If you're moving down the highway at seventy miles per hour on a clear, bright, sunny day with very little traffic, you might think you're making good progress and being very productive. In reality, if your destination lies somewhere *behind* you, in the opposite direction, your activity is actually counterproductive. In this case, going faster or working harder will take you even farther away from your goal or destination than you currently are. Someone who has pulled off to the side of the road and is not moving at all is actually making more progress, or being more productive, than you are.

Just because you're moving, it does not mean you're moving in the right direction.

Ultimate Productivity is only applicable as it relates to your personalized success and your individual mission toward that destiny. Sometimes in the midst of frantic activity, the most productive thing you can do is stop, take a deep breath, and ask yourself several questions.

1. What is it that I'm really trying to accomplish?
2. Do I *really* want to accomplish this?
3. Will this activity move me toward that end result?
4. Is there a better way to get from here to there than the way I am currently pursuing?

In a ready, aim, fire world, too often we overlook the *ready* and *aim* portions of the equation. There's only one good reason to pursue any activity, and that is because it's the most productive and efficient way to accomplish your mission of moving toward your personal success goal.

Not long ago, I had an opportunity to train a team of salespeople. These individuals were engaged in commission selling from cold calls and referrals. They had no responsibilities other than to sell their product. When I arrived on the scene, I first spent most of my time listening and observing their activity.

Too often, outside consultants come into a situation and perform ready, fire, aim consulting. Before you seek anyone's opinion, make sure they understand your unique success goal and the mission you have undertaken to get from here to there. Otherwise, you will get some great advice that may rapidly take you even farther than you already are from where you want to be.

As I observed these individual salespeople, they all appeared to be working very hard. For the most part, they arrived at the office early, engaged in frantic activity, and—by and large—stayed late into the workday. After gathering the information I needed, I called them all together and asked some questions.

1. How many hours a week do you work?
2. Are you working hard?

Their answers were quite revealing. The average salesperson felt they were working about forty-five to fifty hours a week, and they all assured me they were working extremely hard. Then I asked another simple question: What is your job here?

In unison they responded that their job was to sell their company's product. When I asked how they could accomplish this other than by talking to prospects on the phone or in person, it got very quiet.

So then I gave them the good news: They could all make more money by generating more sales—and only working fifteen hours a week. This was greeted with great skepticism.

I gave them each a discount store stopwatch and told them to keep their watches in their jacket pockets or purses during the workday. Anytime they were actually engaged in talking to a prospect about their company's products or services, they were to click the watch on; when they were done, they were to click the watch off until they began talking to another potential customer. I told them that once they had reached fifteen hours of productive work time in the week, as indicated by their stopwatch, they were done until next week.

Since I had already approved this with their supervisor, they were elated to find out they only had to work fifteen hours per week. What they didn't realize was

Never confuse activity with productivity. As you look at your daily, weekly, and monthly calendars, review each item and ask yourself the question, is this *activity* or *productivity*?

Learn to work smarter, not harder; quicker, not more hurried; and productively, not just actively.

that the average salesperson in that organization had actually only been working around five hours a week, and they had been wasting approximately forty hours a week in nonproductive activity.

A few months after they implemented this stopwatch productivity system, I got some feedback on the results. Approximately a third of the salespeople were breaking not only their own previous records but many of the company's sales records. About the same number were still working forty-five hours a week in their old manner, which you and I now understand meant a mere five productive hours a week. And, finally, a third of the salespeople had quit; they could not handle the unstructured freedom and responsibility of Ultimate Productivity.

The top third of the sales force was only coming into the office a few hours each day. They were efficiently and productively establishing new customers, and then spending time with their families, fishing, or improving their golf game. Since their sales numbers were astounding to management, no one cared how many or how few hours they spent in the office.

Your professional workday is about creating productivity, not generating activity designed to convince someone that you're working. I realize that it is hard to define every job in every field in absolute terms of activity versus productivity, but you know better than anyone else when you're making a difference and when you're just treading water for appearances' sake.

One of my heroes and mentors is the legendary ninety-seven year-old coach, John Wooden. You have heard it said that some wise people have forgotten more than anyone else knows. This would be true of Coach Wooden except for the fact that at nearly a hundred, he still hasn't forgotten anything.

In the totally measurable, definable world of big-time college basketball, Coach Wooden has more championships and has created more success than anyone, ever. He dominated the college basketball landscape in a way that has never been equaled before or since.

He recruited and cultivated players such as Kareem Abdul-Jabbar, Bill Walton, and countless college and future NBA stars. Coach Wooden has a phrase he shared with his players that I believe defines Ultimate Productivity for us all. Whenever he had a player who was not getting into position fast enough, he would repeat the phrase, "Be quick, but don't hurry."

As simple as this may seem, it can define the difference between your success and your failure. In Coach Wooden's terms, being quick means moving efficiently and under control toward your destination. Hurrying means being out of control and running with reckless abandon.

Being quick will get you into position to win. Hurrying will simply tire you out on the road to inevitable failure. Quickness is a state of mind. Hurrying is a state of activity.

Remember to never confuse activity with productivity. As you look at your daily, weekly, and monthly calendar, review each item and ask yourself the question, is this *activity* or *productivity*? This can only be judged in light of your firmly-established success goal and the mission you are on to take you there.

If you will learn to work smarter, not harder; quicker and not more hurried; and productively, not simply more actively, you will begin to live a life of Ultimate Productivity, full of peace, serenity, joy, and success beyond your wildest dreams.

NOTES:

CHAPTER FIVE

CUSTOMIZING:
FULFILLING YOUR UNIQUE POTENTIAL

I am an optimist. I believe that the biggest dream you ever had in your life is alive and well, and the only thing you have to do to activate it and eventually live it is create Ultimate Productivity through motivation, communication, and implementation. You have everything you need to live out your dreams. Your goal would not have been put inside of you unless you had the capacity to achieve it.

Having said that, just as your goal is totally unique to you in the way you define success, and just as your mission to pursue that goal is yours alone, the tools, skills, and talents you bring to the task are also completely unique.

One of the challenges with most success books, courses, or philosophies is the fact that some well-meaning person who may be successful is telling you how he or she succeeded, but really has no idea how *you* should succeed. My goal in both this book and the Ultimate Productivity Profile I have set up to help individuals and corporations find their unique path, is to equip you to assess your own unique skill set in order to fulfill your own mission on the way to your defined success. You can take the Ultimate Productivity Profile, free of charge, at www.UltimateProductivity.com by entering your access code: 586404.

As a blind person for more than two decades, I have had to come to grips with the fact that I cannot do things the way I used to do them. If you were to poll a number of blind people concerning the greatest limitations resulting from their disability, I believe many of them would mention two things: reading and driving. Both are perceived to be visual skills, and blind people suffer from their inability to engage in these activities.

In reality, when you understand Ultimate Productivity, reading is not about visually seeing words on a page, and driving is not about operating a vehicle. Reading is the pursuit of information, and driving is simply a matter of getting from point A to point B.

As I explained previously, when I could read words on a page, I don't believe I ever read a book cover to cover; but now, thanks to a high-speed tape player and recordings from the National Library for the Blind, I literally read a book every day.

I have never met a person who has read more books than I have. There are probably people who have, but I simply have never met them. I know that I would enjoy meeting such people, because the act of reading a book a day for over two decades has so expanded my world that I would love to meet people whose world has been expanded to a greater extent than mine.

With respect to driving, I have not operated a vehicle since the day I rear-ended a parked police car I didn't see. This is a bittersweet tale that I will save for another venue, but suffice it to say, that experience ended my active operation of a vehicle more than thirty years ago. But thanks to chauffer-driven limousines, as well as first-class and private air travel, I have gone anywhere around the world I have wanted to go, and look forward to traveling even more in the future.

One must always remember that there is more than one way to skin a cat as my grandmother always told me.

Keep your goal in mind and realize that your mission is merely a way to get your goal. Your goal should never waver or be altered, but your mission to reach that goal and the methods you employ should be totally flexible and constantly scrutinized in the light of Ultimate Productivity.

I am told that each year, several million quarter-inch drill bits are sold in hardware stores and tool outlets around the world. Yet I can safely say that no one ever really wanted a quarter-inch drill bit, though millions of people buy them. What they really want is a quarter-inch hole. If there were another method developed to magically create quarter-inch holes in any substance, I submit to you that the million-drill-bit-a-year market would dry up overnight.

Examine your expectations, and you will find that somewhere along the way you came to expect the life you are experiencing at this moment.

Please remember that we always find what we are looking for. If you seek to have a great day, find a new opportunity, or meet the person who will make the difference in your personal or professional life, it will happen. On the other hand, if you get up tomorrow morning looking for a dull, boring day, the same old regimen, and people who drain you of your energy instead of building you up toward your personal goal, this is, indeed, what you will find.

I hate to be the one to tell you this, but if you haven't figured it out already, it's time you knew that life is not fair. Life is great, it's grand, and it's wonderful, but it is not fair. In this life, we don't always get what we want. We don't always get what we need. We don't always get what we deserve. And we don't always even get what we earn. But we will, inevitably and unerringly, get exactly what we expect.

Never take advice from anyone who doesn't already have what you want.

If your life today does not look like you want it to in every facet of your existence, simply examine your expectations, and you will find that somewhere along the way you came to expect the life you are experiencing at this moment. That may be somewhat startling and disturbing to you, but take heart. If those expectations have brought you here, the expectations you will build and nurture through Ultimate Productivity will take you anywhere you want to go.

Recently, I read a book by a well-meaning Ph.D. purporting to tell readers how to become millionaires. Yet on close examination, not only was this particular Ph.D. *not* a millionaire, but—thanks to the indiscriminate use of credit cards—he had a *negative* net worth. This did not, however, stop him from telling unsuspecting readers the single and true path to becoming a millionaire. Even so, always remember: Whether it's me or anyone else whose thoughts you are reading or listening to, never take advice from anyone who doesn't have what you want.

Recent statistics tell us that there are more than 9 million millionaires in the United States, and I can assure you that there are 9 million ways to reach that goal. They are all valid—but they are *not* interchangeable or transferable.

Michael Jordan found his way to becoming a multimillionaire through being arguably the greatest basketball player ever. In the prime of his career, he decided to pursue becoming a baseball player. His best efforts resulted in Michael Jordan becoming a mediocre minor league baseball player. While it is remarkable that he could achieve even that status in baseball, it is exceedingly obvious that Michael Jordan's path to success was through basketball and, had he only ever played baseball and never explored other avenues and paths to success, you and I would have never heard the name Michael Jordan.

There is a unique path for you and me that will take us down a road where we find power, pleasure, and passion in the ongoing pursuit of our personal success. No matter how hard Michael Jordan might have worked in playing baseball, he would have never reached his personal success or Ultimate Productivity without getting off the baseball road and back onto the basketball road that led him to fame, fortune, and success.

Before you change your tires, tune up your car, and try to get in the fast lane, be sure you're on the *right* road going the *right* direction that will take you to your personal success.

NOTES:

CHAPTER SIX

PASSION:
THE CAUSE AND EFFECT

Before you and I make the quantum leap into motivation, communication, and implementation, which are the engines of Ultimate Productivity, we have to take a brief detour to confirm that you are on track with your personalized definition of success and your customized mission. Unless these elements fit you perfectly, you cannot reach your destination.

The only thing that will make you succeed is to create more value by utilizing Ultimate Productivity. If you are going to go through the fire of achievement, you've got to make sure you're on the exclusive road that will take you to your personal destination. The only way to gauge your accuracy in this area is to examine your passion.

I have been privileged to meet and work with some of the greatest people of the twentieth and now the twenty-first century either onstage, on television, or in interviews for my columns and books. Each of these people has reached the pinnacle in his or her arena of business, sports, politics, social change, or the world of entertainment.

These ultimate achievers come in many shapes and sizes, and there is only one element that I have been able to discern that they all have in common, without fail: an unwavering and burning *passion* for the personal goals they pursue.

My very first interview broadcast on the Narrative Television Network was with legendary movie star Katharine Hepburn. Ms. Hepburn was a pioneer in the movie industry and received acclaim that was unparalleled both from her audiences and her peers. We had several conversations after the interview, and I was in communication with her up until several months prior to her passing.

I will never forget the feeling as a novice interviewer of sitting down that first time to talk with Katharine Hepburn. She was intimidating to me, to say the least, but totally down-to-earth and unassuming. Her answer to one of my questions remains indelibly etched in my mind.

I asked, "Miss Hepburn, if you had not found your way into show business as a movie actress, what field do you feel you would have pursued throughout your life?"

She considered my question for a moment and then responded hesitantly, "I'm not exactly sure what I would have done, but I hope I would have gone into medicine or some healing profession."

Then, with that unwavering degree of certainty that movie fans came to love, she continued emphatically, "If I had not been able to make a living as an actress, I would have had to have found another way to sustain myself as I acted to support my habit, because I act out of an innate need to be an actress."

This kind of passion will sustain you just as it did Katharine Hepburn through the trials and triumphs of pursuing your mission to reach your personal success. Everyone who works hard faces challenges and difficulties. But the ones who prevail are those who are pursuing their own passion.

That reminds me of a story that I often share from the arena stage at events around the world.

Once upon a time, there were two ancient tribes of people that lived in close proximity to one another. One tribe lived in a lush valley near a swiftly flowing river that sustained the tribe and their crops and livestock year-round. The valley people lived an agrarian lifestyle of planting, cultivating, and harvesting throughout the seasons, year after year.

The second ancient tribe lived in the high-up mountains, just below the snow line, where they dwelled in caves and sustained themselves through hunting for meat and furs. The mountain tribe prospered as they taught ensuing generations of their young people the arts of hunting and trapping.

The two ancient tribes lived in different worlds. They rarely even sighted one another, even though they lived less than a day's travel on foot from each other.

As often happens when two societies or groups of people don't communicate, the two tribes began to fear each other and be suspicious of the other. When human beings fail to communicate and understand one another, they always assume the worst to be true.

Then, one day, a group of misguided youths from the mountain tribe strayed beyond their normal hunting grounds. As teenagers will often do, without thinking they acted. These teenagers took a young baby that was sleeping on a pallet near the river where its mother and the other ladies of the valley tribe were washing clothes.

Before they realized it, the teenagers from the mountain tribe were running along the path through the woods that led back to their mountain home, with the women from the valley tribe in hot pursuit. Soon the mountain kidnappers had gone beyond the point of no return, so they went to their cave dwellings with the baby they had kidnapped.

But they hadn't kidnapped just *any* baby. This was the infant son of the chief of the valley tribe.

That very night, the valley tribe held an emergency council meeting around the bonfire. The chief implored his greatest warriors to climb up the mountain and bring back his baby.

At daybreak, the best and strongest warriors from the valley tribe headed up the mountain in pursuit of their chief's son. They were brave and determined but were not accustomed to the mountain terrain, and by sundown they returned dejectedly to the valley campsite and their forlorn chief.

Your personal success goal had better be fully in line with your deepest passion.

With the last rays of the setting sun, the chief and the people of the valley tribe spotted a lone figure coming down the mountain that their warriors had been unable to climb. As the figure approached, it was revealed to be the chief's wife, holding her baby son in her arms.

There was great rejoicing throughout the tribe, and when the celebration subsided, the chief asked his wife in the hearing of all those assembled, "How is it that you, my wife, could climb that mountain and return with our child, when our best and bravest warriors failed?"

She smiled and replied with an answer that rings true for you and me: "It wasn't their baby."

Your personal success goal had better be fully in line with your deepest passion. The fact that your mother wants you to go to college, your spouse wants you to lose weight, or your boss wants you to produce more doesn't matter when we are considering Ultimate Productivity as it relates to your mission and your personal success through motivation, communication, and implementation.

Motivation, communication, and implementation represent powerful tools, but they will only work for you if it's your baby. You will know, deep down, whether it's your baby if you have the passion and the fire inside of you to get up that mountain of your personal success.

Few people ever find and pursue their true passion, so it's easier to see daily examples around us of people mired down in mediocrity, far removed from their personal success and passion.

I once worked with a gentleman who could barely drag himself to work thirty to forty-five minutes late each day, and somehow slog through his day's tasks in slow motion. He was tired, depressed, and dejected every day, and many around him questioned whether he would get out of bed and do it again the next morning. But then, one day, he asked me to go fishing, and I discovered an amazing lesson about passion, courtesy of this gentleman.

The same guy who arrived each morning in a zombie state around 10 a.m. told me he would be picking me up for our fishing trip on Saturday at 3 a.m. I'm an early riser. Most mornings, I'm already listening to my books on tape by 4:15 or 4:30, but 3 a.m. is an hour I rarely experience. Yet the prospect of observing my under energetic friend at that forsaken hour intrigued me, so on Saturday morning at 3:00 sharp, when his truck pulled into my driveway, I got into the cab of his truck expecting the worst.

I received the surprise of my life when I was greeted by one of the most enthusiastic, energetic, passionate people I had ever met. By 4:30, we were wading thigh-deep in a freezing stream, and he was a nonstop bundle of joy all day. With only a few brief breaks for food and water, he was a constant fishing machine, on fire until long after sunset. As we drove home, he gave me an excited, blow-by-blow recap of his entire thirteen hours of fishing that day.

As we approached my house and he dropped me off, it dawned on me that we had found his passion, or his "power groove."

When I was in high school, I thought I wanted to be a professional football player, but when I was diagnosed with the condition that eventually robbed me of my eyesight, I knew I would never make the NFL; so I became a competitive weight lifter and actually won a national championship for my weight class and age division.

George Burns once told me that if you love your job, you never have to work a day in your life.

Among weight lifters, it is well known that there is such a thing as a power groove, which is a very narrow range of motion in which weight lifters are significantly stronger than the average person. But they also know that if the strongest weight lifter in the world gets just a few inches out of his power groove, his strength diminishes geometrically.

Our professional and personal lives are the same way. If we live, move, and have our being within the realm of our passion, we are unbeatable; but if we get out of our power grooves, like the passionate fisherman on an average workday in the office, we are doomed to failure.

George Burns told me that if you love your job, you never have to work a day in your life.

Late in his career, golf legend Lee Trevino gave me the opportunity to interview him. During our conversation, he told me that after many consecutive weeks of playing competitive golf he would come home, throw his golf clubs in the garage, and tell anyone who would listen, "I'm never going to play golf again." But after a good night's sleep, he was generally rummaging around in the garage, loading up his golf clubs, and heading out to get on a golf course somewhere. He shrugged and sheepishly explained, "Jim, I just love to play golf."

Probably the highlight of my celebrity interviews was the afternoon I spent with Frank Sinatra. No one before or since has dominated show business for half a century like Frank Sinatra did. There was an amazing energy around Mr. Sinatra.

He and his entourage had taken over the top several floors of a major hotel complex in preparation for a concert he was doing that night. The street had been barricaded for a number of blocks around the hotel, and security was extremely tight. News helicopters were flying around the hotel, and it was an amazing environment.

I remember commenting to Mr. Sinatra and several of his people that they had created quite a stir in Dallas. A bit perplexed, Mr. Sinatra asked one of his confidants, "Do you know what this guy's talking about?"

The nearest bodyguard/assistant replied, "Yes, sir, I do. But you probably don't."

Then it dawned on me. For his entire adult life, Frank Sinatra had never been anywhere that wasn't experiencing the same Frank Sinatra effect that Dallas was experiencing that day. He thought the chaos was normal.

Later, as I interviewed Mr. Sinatra, I found that he epitomized passion in several ways. When I asked him, as a movie star, recording artist, TV personality, and so much more, how he would like to be remembered, he said he would like to be remembered as a guy telling a simple story through a song that made people feel things.

We had a great interview, and afterward, as I was getting ready to leave, he called out to me with words I'll never forget. "Hey, kid. I hope you live to be a hundred years old, and the last thing you ever hear is me singing you a song."

May you and I similarly find our own passions in life.

NOTES:

CHAPTER SEVEN

DISCOVERY:
THREE POWERFUL TOOLS

In the entire continuum from first becoming aware that you have choices and can act on them, to completing your mission and living your dreams through your personal success, there are many rungs on the ladder.

I want to congratulate you for defining success on your own terms, establishing a mission from where you are to where you want to be, and examining your destination in light of your passion. You're well on your way to living out your dreams, but it's important to realize that many people have had dreams, set goals, and launched into a mission. The greatest disconnects along the road to success are the practical steps that involve *motivation*, *communication*, and *implementation*.

You may have a lifelong dream or a ten-year goal, and these things are valid, but it all comes down to taking that first step. You've heard it said that a journey of a thousand miles begins with a single step. I'll go one further and submit to you that a journey of a thousand miles is nothing more than a series of single steps, but if you stop or take a detour on any one of those steps, you will not reach your destination.

> A journey of a thousand miles is nothing more than a series of single steps, but if you stop or take a detour on any one of those steps, you will not reach your destination.

Through my speeches, syndicated column, and books, I have the privilege of meeting and corresponding with countless people who have lofty goals and worthwhile dreams. They have a plan that takes them far into the future, but unfortunately, they don't have a plan that takes into account this day, this hour, or this moment.

Those of you who are familiar with my work, or have read another of my dozen or so books, are most likely familiar with my novel *The Ultimate Gift* or the Twentieth Century Fox movie based on it. For some reason that story of an elderly man's desire to pass on his knowledge and wisdom, and not just his riches, has resonated with many millions of people around the world.

In the movie, legendary actor James Garner plays the part of an elderly gentleman named Red Stevens. Knowing he is nearing the end of his life, Stevens leaves behind twelve videotaped messages for his grandson, dealing with twelve pivotal life lessons as he sees them.

In the aftermath of the successful movie and millions of *Ultimate Gift* books in print, people ask me which of the twelve gifts is most important in life. When you consider the gifts of money, work, friends, family, love, and several others, it's hard to pick just one. But if I were forced to pick the most important gift as it relates to achieving your personal success, it would invariably be the Gift of a Day.

In the Gift of a Day, you begin to recognize that, at best, life is very short. Even if you live to what we consider to be an old age, it flies by in the blink of an eye. Having a successful life is nothing more

> Yesterday is a canceled check, and tomorrow is little more than a promissory note. Today is cash. It is real, it is tangible, and you and I have to spend it wisely.

than stringing together a series of successful years. A successful year is simply a matter of laying down twelve successful months. A successful month takes nothing more than the establishment of four successful weeks, and a successful week is made up of a series of successful days. But when it's all said and done, the only day that matters is today. Yesterday is a canceled check, and tomorrow is little more than a promissory note. Today is cash. It is real, it is tangible, and you and I have to spend it wisely.

Every day is a gift, and how you use it brings you either one day closer to or one day farther from your goal.

For seven or eight years, I have written a weekly column that is read by people through newspapers, magazines, and online publications around the world. My column is entitled Winners' Wisdom, and each week I try to deliver just that—a piece of wisdom that, if applied, will create winners. Every one of these columns ends with a single phrase: "Today's the Day!"

When my publisher put together a compilation of these columns in book form, they gave it the title *Today's the Day*, simply because you can read about, hear about, or learn of wisdom, but unless you apply it, it doesn't matter. It's simply knowledge with no energy. Once you apply that knowledge, it becomes wisdom, and the only time you can apply wisdom in your life is today.

I'm not as interested in the specifics of your personal goal or your mission to get there as I am in your activity today. Every day is a gift, and how you use it brings you either one day closer to or one day farther from your goal. If you work like, act like, and have an attitude like someone who is on his way to achieving your personal goal, you are already successful.

The great hotel baron Conrad Hilton was once asked when he knew he would be successful. He told the reporter he knew he would be successful when he was still penniless and sleeping on a park bench, because he was doing the things it took to reach his personal success.

Today is all you have to invest in your future. If you're going to succeed, you're going to do so by employing the success elements of motivation, communication, and implementation. Everyone who has ever succeeded has done so with these principles, whether or not they defined them in the terms that you and I are defining them.

Motivation is the fuel that makes your mission toward your personal success possible. It is the first thing we get when we come into this life and the last thing that slips away as we leave. We do everything we do—good or bad—because for one reason or another, we are motivated to do so. Recognizing that today is the only thing you have to invest toward your success, if you haven't been investing wisely, you have to change your motivation.

Communication is the way you define and share your mission and personal success for yourself and those around you. No one has ever succeeded by themselves. If someone tells you they have never failed at anything, you can confidently let them know that, if nothing else, at a minimum they failed to recognize the contribution of others.

Unless you can communicate your goals, you really don't own them, and you haven't firmly established them in your own mind. Great educators will tell you that the best way to learn a subject is to teach it. The very process of communicating a lesson drives it deeper into your mind and into your soul.

You will need to build a success team. They cannot draw on your passion. They can only draw on what you communicate. What you feel, think, or believe is meaningless unless you can share it. This can only be done through communication.

Implementation is putting your thoughts, dreams, passions, mission, and personal success goals into action. In our world, when it's all said and done, there's a lot more said than done. You will not live out your dreams because you meant to act today or because you intended to take the right steps. Your best intentions are meaningless. You will reap the rewards of your Ultimate Productivity.

If you meant to cook dinner but didn't, you will be hungry. If you intended to light the fire, but you failed to act, you will be cold. And, just as certainly, if you don't implement your mission on a daily basis, you will fail.

I wish I could give you the blueprint for your own motivation, communication, and implementation; however, these elements are as individual to you as your fingerprints. Fortunately, you hold the keys to these blueprints of your own motivation, communication, and implementation and those members of your success team you will be drawing toward you.

You may think you're motivating an associate by drawing attention to her accomplishments in front of a vast audience. In reality, that may be terrifying, demoralizing, and demotivating to that individual. In this case, your best intentions will be taking you farther away from your intended goal. You may think you're communicating your mission to those around you who have accepted the task of creating Ultimate

Productivity and success; however, if you're communicating in English and they all speak French, or if you're communicating in writing and they can't read, you're not going to succeed.

Remember, as a blind person I can't see the words, but I read more than anyone I know via audio books. If you were trying to communicate with me but insisted on doing it through black on white, ink on paper, you and I could not succeed.

And, finally, if you are trying to implement yourself or engage those around you in beginning a task, you've got to understand how everyone, collectively, achieves their maximum performance in order to create Ultimate Productivity.

If you and your team were committed to the task of rebuilding and restoring the Statue of Liberty as was done several years ago, you would have to motivate your team to give their best efforts to preserve this symbol of our freedom and all it means. You would also have to communicate your passion for the project and your instructions for everyone involved. But unless you could implement, nothing that had gone before would really matter.

If you and your team decided that you were going to begin working at 6:00 a.m., but then you discovered that the first ferry did not run to Liberty Island until 9:00 a.m., you simply couldn't implement.

More people fail due to misguided motivation, chaotic communication, and inappropriate implementation than anything else.

NOTES:

CHAPTER EIGHT

HONEST ASSESSMENT:
GETTING INTO POSITION

As an athlete, businessperson, and success speaker, I have had the privilege of studying winners and losers for several decades. The difference between winners and losers is relatively minor on the productivity side and overwhelming on the reward side.

As I have studied success and those who make it happen in the corporate arena, investment field, and the world of entrepreneurship, it resurfaces time after time that the winning edge invariably happens when the elements of motivation, communication, and implementation all come together. For this reason, I have put together this book and an Ultimate Productivity Profile that entrepreneurs, investors, and those in the corporate world utilize to bring these critical elements into focus. To take the Ultimate Productivity Profile—free of charge—visit www.UltimateProductivity.com and enter the following access code: 586404.

Although you have established your own driving definition of success (your specific mission to get you from here to there, as well as the passion that will carry you through over the long haul), without the practical elements of motivation, communication, and implementation, you will be all dressed up with nowhere to go. These elements are vital to everyone but are individual in the way they must be brought to bear upon your specific situation.

Let's say you are getting into your dress-for-success mode and want a custom suit made so you can look and feel your best. No matter how motivated your tailor may be; no matter how much you communicate to him or her the style, fabric, and design you want; and no matter how willing and able your tailor is to begin implementing the process, without knowing and understanding your specific measurements, you don't have a chance of ever getting a top-of-the-line tailor-made suit.

Many leaders around the world have been intricately involved with the development of the Ultimate Productivity Profile, which allows individuals and those they work with to understand their own specific strengths as it relates to motivation, communication, and implementation.

One of my great influences in developing the Ultimate Productivity Profile has been legendary coach John Wooden. No one has ever been more successful at putting together a winning team. He did it year after year, with different circumstances and different players. Coach Wooden helped me understand that motivation, communication, and implementation are imperative, but you must work with each player and every team differently.

If you are committed to a certain vehicle or route instead of being committed to success itself, your odds of living out your dreams or experiencing your destiny are very low.

Some players are motivated by a pat on the back. Other players need their pat a little lower and a bit harder. Some players need verbal communication, and others have to see a diagram of the play drawn out on a board. Some players implement best with long, rigorous practices, while others need several sessions a day.

There are many ways, styles, and vehicles that can get you to your destination. But if you are committed to a certain vehicle or route instead of being committed to success itself, your odds of living out your dreams or experiencing your destiny are very low.

I travel by plane numerous times each month. Once, when talking to a pilot, I was extremely concerned to learn that, during a two-hour flight, he is off course the vast majority of the time. When a flight plan is filed and the pilot logs all of the trip information into the computer, the onboard computer virtually maps out the perfect flight from the plane's point of origin to its intended destination. Unfortunately, from the takeoff to the landing, that plane is constantly either too high, too low, or off course to the left or right. If you fly regularly, you'll be thankful to know, as I was, that the onboard computer and the pilot constantly correct the course.

If pilots were only committed to the computerized model instead of being committed to their destinations, the minute they got off course they would simply circle around, land at the airport where they just took off, and try again later.

No one who ever succeeded got there exactly the way they thought they would. Even if things go exactly according to your plan, conditions between here and there are changing constantly.

Coach Wooden realized there are certain absolutes in the game of basketball. For example, you've got to score more points than the other team during the time allotted for the game. But beyond that, there are as many ways to motivate, communicate, and implement as there are players who have ever played the game.

Success is never a one-size-fits-all proposition. It is a custom-tailored, one-of-a-kind, magnificent suit, lovingly made with no one in mind other than you.

Coach Wooden had a specific coaching pattern and a certain method for deciding on the roles each player was to fulfill. But then he recruited a player named Lew Alcindor. Not only was Lew taller and quicker, but he also possessed skills that were different from virtually anyone who had ever played the game. The goal of winning by scoring more points than the other team in the prescribed time for the game never changed; however, Coach Wooden realized that, within his system, he needed to be flexible enough to utilize the tremendous talent and potential of this new player.

Alcindor went on to become one of the greatest college basketball players of all time, and Coach Wooden led his team to national championships because he adapted the way he motivated, communicated, and implemented with Lew Alcindor and the other members of that team in a way that brought out their Ultimate Productivity. Incidentally, Lew Alcindor also rewrote the record books in the NBA and became known as Kareem Abdul-Jabbar.

The people in your office or on your team have as much talent and potential as Kareem Abdul-Jabbar did as a basketball player, but you're going to have to understand who they are and how you can produce Ultimate Productivity through the unique blend of motivation, communication, and implementation that suits them. Success is never a one-size-fits-all proposition. It is a custom-tailored, one-of-a-kind, magnificent suit, lovingly made with no one in mind other than you.

As a blind person myself, and as the president of the Narrative Television Network that makes movies, television, and educational programming accessible for our nation's 13 million blind and visually impaired people, I have long been involved in the field of special education. But for many years, this field did not exist. Students with disabilities that did not allow them to function in the expected, standard way in the classroom simply did not receive an education. Then, as specific disabilities became more understood within the medical and educational communities, the field of special education was born.

In the beginning, students who could not function in the standard, or what was thought of as "normal," way were said to have a "learning disability." The term *learning disabled* permeated the special-education arena for many years. No doubt, this made opportunities limited for untold numbers of students who were not given the customized tools and specific encouragement needed to reach their potential.

More recently, a new term has emerged in special education. Today, students once identified as "learning disabled" are now known to have a *learning difference*, not a "disability." The labeling alone has made a huge impact, because we all have a tendency to live up to labels and the expectations attached to them. *Learning disabled* denotes a student with a disability or a problem that does not allow him or her to function up to par. But *learning difference* indicates a unique person that may simply need to take an alternative route to get to the same destination—or possibly even a greater destination—than his or her peers. *Learning disability* defines a deficiency in the student. *Learning difference* alerts the teacher to seek new ways to motivate, communicate, and implement with this individual.

You can also apply this reasoning to yourself and those you work with. If you try to work exactly like those around you—or try to make everyone around you perform exactly like you—you will never reach your own definition of success through Ultimate Productivity.

Hammers, screwdrivers, and wrenches are all irreplaceable tools for a carpenter, but they are hardly interchangeable. The best carpenter in the world will have his productivity diminished or halted completely if he tries to drive nails with a screwdriver. If Coach Wooden had tried to make Kareem Abdul-Jabbar play point guard and dribble the ball down the court, while the five-foot-ten point guard played center, I don't believe the championship banners displayed at UCLA would be there today.

At my company, Narrative Television Network, I believe we have the best team in the world. I hope you feel that way about your team. NTN has logistical people, accounting people, technical TV production people, and creative people. They are all vital, and I believe they are the very best at what they do, but they are hardly interchangeable.

It seems to be a universal law that the more someone excels in one area, the less competence he or she has in others. Ultimate Productivity in any specific field requires talent, hard work, and dedication. By necessity, the farther you climb up the ladder in one area, the less altitude you're able to achieve in others.

As I mentioned previously, I was a weight lifter. Weight lifting is a competitive sport in the Olympics. In the summer Olympics, there are also sprinters, gymnasts, and swimmers. All are elite, high-performance, Ultimate Productivity athletes within their own fields; but if you have a weight lifter competing in a swimming event, or a gymnast entered in the weight-lifting competition, you are more likely to experience comedy than competitive drama.

As I dictate these words, they are being typed into a computer by an extremely talented grammarian, Dorothy Thompson, without whom no one would have read even one of my books or weekly syndicated columns. I am quite certain of this, because I don't know how to type and, as a consumer of audio books, I have no knowledge or understanding of spelling or punctuation. Yet, thanks to Dorothy, this has not kept me from selling millions and millions of books.

Downstairs in our building, we have four state-of-the-art digital TV editing studios. I don't even know how to turn the equipment on, but I still run a successful television network. In fact, I have received an Emmy award from the National Academy of Television Arts and Sciences recognizing NTN's engineering expertise—yet I don't even know the names of the various pieces of machinery in our own facilities. Please don't tell the Academy!

If you are going to become the master of your own success goal by utilizing Ultimate Productivity through motivation, communication, and implementation, you must pursue your passion by doing the things in which *you* excel. You're also going to need to recognize these same elements in everyone around you so that each player on your team is a world-class champion in his or her own area.

You become unstoppable, and your personalized success goal becomes a certainty, when you establish your own unique profile—and the profiles of those around you—within Ultimate Productivity. If you and every member of your team are functioning within your passion, utilizing your power grooves with total communication and maximum implementation, your life becomes a fully fueled rocket ship that will launch you into a universe far beyond your wildest dreams.

It all begins with motivation.

NOTES:

CHAPTER NINE

MOTIVATION:
A MAGIC MACHINE

Whether you are pursuing your personal goal through the corporate world, entrepreneurship, or investing, you will have to understand how motivation, communication, and implementation relate to you and everyone around you if you are to achieve Ultimate Productivity.

Oftentimes, though, the hardest person to understand is oneself. Too many of us have a tendency to live in the past, because we know all of our own shortcomings and keep repeating to ourselves all of our past stumbles and continually drag them into our future.

But we are not the persons we were in the past—unless we choose to be. Even if you have experienced multiple failures before, you are no longer that person, because you have the wisdom and the knowledge that come from those experiences. You have heard it said that insanity is continually doing the same thing but expecting a different result. Conversely, wisdom dictates that if a certain behavior has brought us failure, we simply need to change the behavior in order to alter our future.

You have heard it said that insanity is continually doing the same thing but expecting a different result. Conversely, wisdom dictates that if a certain behavior has brought us failure, we simply need to change the behavior in order to alter our future.

Once you have identified and connected for yourself how to best utilize motivation, communication, and implementation in your individual world, you've got to be committed to continually monitoring the changes in your own life and how they impact you.

Shakespeare may have said it best when he wrote, "To thine own self be true." Like all great wisdom, this is exceedingly simple to say and unbelievably difficult to master. But you'll be happy to know that you do not have to achieve perfection in order to enjoy your personal success. Some of my favorite baseball players have gone into the Hall of Fame by failing at the plate more times than they succeeded.

Donald Trump has always meant a lot to me and is an excellent role model and mentor. I have learned a great deal from him, both by watching his success and his setbacks. When Donald succeeds, he does it on a grand scale. He does the same when he stumbles. Yet when he does fall, he gets up, brushes himself off, and begins again—just as you and I must do.

In the process of mastering motivation on your way to your personal success through Ultimate Productivity, it is critical to determine the most productive way to constantly motivate not only yourself but also every individual with whom you work. Remember, whether you spend your workday locked in a small office in your basement, typing on a computer, or in the middle of a megacorporation surrounded by several thousand colleagues, you work both with yourself and with others. You've got to pull the maximum motivational trigger for everyone, and it is not a one-size-fits-all proposition.

Let's start with the premise that you probably don't understand what motivates yourself, and you certainly don't get accurate feedback regarding what motivates your colleagues, coworkers, and associates. The higher up the ladder you are and the more imporant you are to those with whom you work, the more difficult it is to get accurate feedback.

If the CEO of a corporation asks everyone in the building how they like his tie on any given day, how often do you think he's going to get truthful, constructive feedback? If he spends considerable time, effort, and money developing a strategy or program to motivate all of his people and then presents it in a company-wide meeting, he is likely to be showered with compliments, and applause, regardless of what they really think.

I have worked with many top corporations and am constantly amazed to discover how little those who make the decisions know about how best to motivate the people for whom they are responsible. People are not exactly lying. They are giving answers and feedback that they feel is in their own enlightened self-interest.

If you're at your family Thanksgiving dinner and, in front of the whole tribe, Aunt Matilda asks you what you think of her baked squash casserole, I suspect that—even if you think Aunt Matilda's casserole tastes like wallpaper paste—you're going to come up with some kind of answer that is at least neutral if not positive.

Just as you want to protect both Aunt Matilda's feelings and your favor with her, your employees want to preserve their jobs, livelihoods, and families' financial security; therefore, it is important to realize that the higher up the ladder you are, and the more important you are to those with whom you work, the more difficult it is to get accurate feedback—especially if you're the boss.

This constraint creates a false environment, where nothing ever changes. If you're going to reach your personal success goal through Ultimate Productivity utilizing motivation, communication, and implementation, you're not only going to have to be honest with yourself and those around you, but you're also going to need to create an environment in which people are comfortable being honest with *you*.

The term *motivation* is among the most misunderstood terms in our business-and-success vocabulary. For years people have labeled me a "motivational" speaker, columnist, or author. While I understand the title and even appreciate their intentions, it is important to note that I don't *motivate* anyone, nor does anyone else. The most you can hope to do is find someone's hot button—something that resonates inside that individual's soul about which he or she is *already* motivated.

Remember, you can never succeed by confusing activity with productivity. If all you want is frantic activity, you can get your people to appear motivated through fear, intimidation, or coercion. You could walk into your office tomorrow and tell everyone, with a threatening tone, that you are going to begin terminating people until the corporate motivation level improves. What you will get is a group of people who will smile, act busy, and probably say, "Yes sir" or "Yes ma'am"—but you have not *motivated* anyone. In fact, you have actually demotivated everyone.

Your intentions to motivate those around you will fail and even be counterproductive if your actions are not specific, targeted, mutually beneficial, and sincere. You may think you're motivating one of your associates by recognizing her birthday and telling her how much she means to you and your organization, but if her birthday was seven and a half months ago, she will be even less motivated than before.

Your motivational efforts have got to be specific to *each person* you seek to motivate. Here's another example.

Many years ago, I am certain a football coach somewhere read that rousing music could motivate his team. So for many years, players suited up while listening to what their coaches thought was motivating. The last time I visited a football locker room before a big game, it was as silent as a morgue. Some of the players were lounging, others were stretching, while still others were reviewing playbooks. But most of the players were wearing headsets attached to their iPods.

I later learned from the trainer that some of the players liked to listen to loud rock music before a game, while others preferred rap, classical, jazz, and every other imaginable style of music. Still other players listened to sound effects, like ocean waves, forest sounds, or simply white noise. And still other players preferred silence.

If you simply assumed one thing was motivating for everyone, you would have failed miserably to motivate and would have actually demotivated many of the players.

One of the things my friend and colleague Zig Ziglar says is that motivation is individualized, and it is in constant demand. But one time, he told me, he met a gentleman who explained to him that he didn't need to go to a motivational meeting, because he had been to so many and had heard it all. Then Zig asked him if he had taken a shower today. Bewildered, the gentleman said yes, he had taken a shower. Zig then told him that motivation was a bit like taking a shower. The shower you took last week, last month, or last year has probably worn off by now.

My university training is in the fields of psychology and sociology. Much of the current thinking would tell us that we human beings do everything we do for one of two reasons: to gain pleasure, or to avoid pain. While these are certainly valid motivators, I would submit that the majority of people you see commuting daily on the freeways, subways, or sidewalks are going back to their jobs—just as they did yesterday and the day before—more out of a sense of habit than any form of motivation. At one point in the past, they may have been motivated by their jobs, or at least they were more motivated about getting a job than starving to death; however, this is far from the motivation that you and I seek to reach our personal success through Ultimate Productivity.

Remember, whether you work in the largest corporation in the world, a small business, or by yourself as an entrepreneur or investor, we all are part of a team, and only those of us who recognize this fact can succeed by achieving Ultimate Productivity.

Your team is much like a jumbo jet airliner. There may be four hundred people on board, all going to the same destination; however, there are as many different motivations for the trip as there are people in the seats. The pilot, co-pilot, and flight attendants are all doing their jobs, but some members of the crew may have a total passion for flying or serving the traveling public, while others are simply marking time, putting in their hours, because they don't know what else to do.

Among the passengers onboard, you might find people going to weddings, funerals, graduations, vacations, moving to or from a new city, or a myriad of other motivating factors. There will be people onboard for whom this flight will be an unforgettable experience because it is taking them to a once-in-a-lifetime event. They may be sitting next to a tired, bored businessperson who is on their fourth or fifth flight of the week.

I have met people who think they are motivated by money, but in reality they are motivated by their perception of what money can do for them in their lives. Money is a poor motivator unless it is attached to the vision of what the money will do for you. Some of the saddest people I know are trying to put more zeroes on their bank statement each month. Unless the pursuit of money is attached to college tuition, comfortable retirement, exciting travel, philanthropic gifts, financial security, or a myriad of other valid utilizations, this pursuit of money is the sign of a serious disease called MORE.

If all you want is more money, but you have not defined a significant use for that money, you are like the guy trying to put more gas in a tank that is already full, in a car that has no destination. A vehicle and fuel are useless if you don't have a personal goal. A nicer vehicle and more fuel will not solve your challenge. You've got to find that personal goal that sends you on a lifelong mission with passion. Then you will have achieved Ultimate Productivity.

Why am I doing what I'm doing in life? If the answer to that question doesn't motivate you and those around you, find something else to do—and quick.

It is hard to imagine that money could even be a motivation for some people. I am proud to say that I consider Steve Forbes among my friends. He is a respected colleague and a valuable example and encourager to me. I cannot imagine Steve Forbes being motivated by money, other than as a means to keep score as he strives to improve himself and his organization.

Steve Forbes was born with more money than most of us will ever have or even imagine. One of the many reasons I admire him is the fact that he recognizes that his role in the world is to provide service and value to his colleagues and customers. He knows that the eventual result of providing this service and creating value in the lives of others is that he and those around him will make more money. But the money, in and of itself, is not a motivator—only what it can do or what it represents.

Most people, individually or corporately, make the mistake of looking at each task or objective as a series of questions. They look at: What are we doing, where are we doing it, who are we doing it with, how are we doing it, and when do we start? These are all critical questions that should be answered right after you answer the question that the motivation portion of Ultimate Productivity demands, which is the overarching question: Why are we doing this? If the answer to that question doesn't motivate you and those around you, find something else to do.

NOTES:

CHAPTER TEN

ESTABLISHING MOTIVATIONAL MIRACLES

I began my business career as a broker for a New York Stock Exchange member firm. I had my own office in a relatively small town and was given the freedom to work independently as if I were an entrepreneur. In that field during the 1980s, there were tremendous promotions run by mutual funds, insurance companies, and large brokerage firms to get people like me to market their investment products and services.

Every few days, I was offered the opportunity to win a trip, a car, a cruise, and every imaginable inducement to capture my attention and that of brokers across the country. This was before the Internet revolutionized the investment and financial planning world. Virtually all of my critical information was printed out on a bulky, noisy, temperamental machine we called the "night wire."

Each morning when I arrived at my office, a printout, often stretching thirty to forty feet long, would be lying on the floor. The printout told brokers across the country what new stock and bond offerings were available, the special contests and promotions that were being held, and the sales performance numbers for individual brokers. It was fascinating to observe which brokers' sales numbers shot up at what times.

I found it comical that Bill or Fred would sell millions of dollars of oil and gas partnerships just to win what I thought was a dumb trip to Chicago. I would laugh to myself, thinking that with a fraction of the commissions they earned for those sales, they could travel around the world; yet somehow a free trip to Chicago had motivated them. I certainly felt that I was not vulnerable to these kinds of tawdry commercial motivational tactics.

Then one morning, we were going over the night wire, and it announced that any broker who sold several million dollars' worth of a new bond offering would receive six prime steaks, packed in dry ice, and a bottle of French champagne, overnighted to the winning broker's office.

By the end of the following day, I had broken all of my own sales records and most of the records for the entire firm before I realized that while I had been making fun of other brokers about their getting hooked by a gimmick, I had done the same thing, only worse. I didn't get a trip to Chicago or anywhere else. I got a box of frozen meat and a bottle of carbonated alcohol.

Then I began to realize that motivation is among the most individualized, personalized human traits. We spend inordinate amounts of time and money tracking what people do, and very little effort and energy determining why they do it.

If the CEO of my firm had called me and asked if I was excited about the possibility of winning a trip to Chicago, I would have immediately responded, "Yes sir." Then I would have done nothing out of the ordinary for the next few days as a result of that promotion. In fact, I probably would have been demotivated, because I would have been thinking about how absurd it was to go out of my way and make an extraordinary effort for a trip I had no interest in taking.

On the other hand, by the next week, brokers across America were all reading their night wires, wondering why in the world I broke records to win a package of frozen steak and champagne that they wouldn't have gone across the street to get for free.

For this reason, I have—in conjunction with some of the greatest performance masters of our time—developed the Ultimate Productivity Profile. This brief survey tool allows people to assess their own motivational triggers as well as those of the people with whom they are associated. The Ultimate Productivity Profile is nonthreatening because there are no right or wrong answers. It simply identifies internal and external factors that cause us to perform. To take the Ultimate Productivity Profile—free of charge—visit www.UltimateProductivity.com and enter the following access code: 586404.

> Honest people will rarely, if ever, lie to you, but at the same time, seldom will they share their deepest, darkest, true feelings with you—assuming they even understand them themselves.

The Ultimate Productivity Profile can give more accurate and detailed information in twenty minutes about how to motivate yourself and those around you than you can get in twenty years of a standard work environment relationship. Remember, honest people will rarely, if ever, lie to you, but at the same time, seldom will they share their deepest, darkest, true feelings with you—assuming they even understand them themselves.

I have a friend and colleague who for many years ran a billion-dollar corporation employing several thousand people. He became legendary by implementing a policy of taking an annual corporate trip. Once a year every employee, from the janitor to the CEO, would be given an all-expense-paid corporate trip for him-/herself and a guest. Employees who had been in the company for ten years or ten minutes were all treated the same. Everybody got the free trip.

It was front-page news every year when four or five 747s flew into town and took all of my friend's employees and guests on an all-expense-paid trip to Las Vegas, Disney World, or another exciting destination.

I remember an enlightening breakfast meeting I had with my friend when I asked how he was able to afford such a corporate extravagance. He shared with me that the trips cost about $1,000 per year for each employee; therefore, he budgeted approximately $20 per week for each member of his entire corporate staff.

When I began to understand the scope of the motivation provided for the cost expended, I was astounded. Imagine if, instead of my friend offering you an all-expense-paid trip for you and a guest to a fantastic location, he told you that you were going to receive an additional $20 a week. If this caught your attention at all, it would probably be demotivating because it might seem like a paltry sum to present to you in recognition for all of your hard work.

On the other hand, my friend's employees were super-motivated, tremendously loyal, and very proud to work for an organization that had a tremendous reputation in the community, because everybody knew that all of those employees got to go on the annual free trip.

It's important to realize that you don't necessarily have to spend more money, more energy, or more time to create more motivation in your life or the lives of those around you. You have to instead find their individual and collective motivational buttons, and push them.

During the mid 1990s, I was invited to tour one of the hottest and fastest-growing dot-com companies of that time. They were experiencing meteoric success, and their biggest challenge was attracting and retaining qualified people to do all the work they were generating. This company had a tremendous amount of cash on hand, a profit picture that would be the envy of any enterprise, and unbelievable positive potential stretching out into the future.

As I arrived for my special tour, I was anticipating a palatial office with plush appointments and state-of-the-art technology. As my assistant and I were escorted into the main lobby, we were nearly struck by a young man in his twenties wearing Bermuda shorts and a tank top, riding a skateboard barefoot, at an unbelievable rate of speed. I was shocked when I realized my host and tour guide didn't even seem to notice this unprecedented behavior within a corporate setting.

Then we were escorted into a huge area where the computer programmers worked. There were basketball goals, a volleyball net, and a trampoline in the middle of computer cubicles that were decorated more like a college dorm than a traditional setting in corporate America. There was loud music blaring, snack trays conveniently and liberally available throughout the work area, and I received a cordial invitation to participate in something they called the Friday beer bash.

I was already beginning to feel a bit like Alice in Wonderland, taking a tour of a world with

> In the world of motivating yourself and those around you, a few people make things happen, a few more watch things happen, but the great multitude of people are unaware that anything even *is* happening.

which I was not familiar, so without thinking, I agreed to attend the aforementioned beer bash.

Apparently, every Friday afternoon, this successful corporation would bring in kegs of beer, hire a local band, and have a function that more resembled a fraternity party than what I had previously thought of as a corporate function. As I was preparing to tell the CEO that I didn't understand what was going on, it dawned on me that, really, I didn't understand his people and what motivated them. I later learned that this particular corporation got more hours of productive work and bottom-line profitability out of each employee than anyone in their industry.

While these tactics would have spelled instant failure in the world of accounting or investment banking, it was an absolute prescription for success within the exploding world of technology at that time.

When I asked the CEO how in the world he had devised such a plan for his people, he chuckled and gave me the answer that became the birth of the Ultimate Productivity Profile. He said, "I asked them."

In the world of motivating yourself and those around you, a few people make things happen, a few more watch things happen, and the great multitude of people are unaware that anything happened.

I'm quite certain that in your personal and professional life, you are extremely busy. We only have twenty-four hours every day and manage to fill each of them. Like me, you probably have a "to do" list. Each day is probably scheduled and filled up to overflowing. Most days, some things have to be carried over to tomorrow's list.

So let's imagine you come into the office on a typical Monday morning and look at all the things you need to accomplish before Friday evening. You probably would be questioning whether you or anybody else could get all of these things done in five short workdays.

Let's say your boss came in and read over your list with you, as well as the lists of all the colleagues with whom you work. Let's further assume that, after reviewing everyone's calendars, the boss said, "I want everyone to get the entire week's activities concluded by noon Wednesday, or else you will suffer the consequences."

You can imagine that a millisecond after the boss exited, there would be wailing, gnashing of teeth, and total outrage regarding the absurd and inhuman demands your boss had put upon you and your coworkers. It would probably approach the low point of motivation for all concerned. It's not hard to imagine that many people might be formulating their letters of resignation and considering their next career moves.

Now imagine that the boss returns in the midst of this motivational desert he has just created and announces, "I'm sorry. I failed to mention a small detail when I told you I wanted you to get an entire week's work done by noon Wednesday or you would suffer the consequences. The consequences for not completing your week's work in half the time will be the fact that you will miss the boat—a cruise ship that will be leaving that afternoon, taking you, your family, and everyone in this corporation that has completed their week's work on an all-expense-paid luxury cruise."

As our theoretical boss made his second exit, I'm quite certain we would find a different environment and a significantly altered motivational climate. Remember, nothing changed between what may have been the worst moment in that corporation's history and the best moment in that corporation's history, except for the motivation provided and the fact that it was communicated.

The results were not possible without the motivation, but the motivation did not exist without communication.

NOTES:

CHAPTER ELEVEN

THE COMMUNICATION CONTRADICTION

We live in the information age, but it is certainly not the communication age. Many people are laboring under the false assumption that if they simply have more information, more details, and more data, there will be accurate and complete communication. In reality, in the world of communication, the less you can say, while still delivering your message, the better off you are.

There is a reason why it is against the law in most areas of the country to go into a crowded building and yell, "Fire!" This is only one simple word, and it's not obscene, demeaning, or derogatory in any way, but the reason we are prohibited from yelling, "Fire!" is because that one word instantly and totally communicates the details surrounding a situation that causes people to act not only immediately but frantically.

Remember, just because you're talking and someone else is listening doesn't mean you are communicating. Communication is the process of getting thoughts, ideas, and concepts from your mind to someone else's. Language, writing, diagrams, and data are all tools to facilitate this transfer, but they can get in the way.

In the world of communication, the less you can say, while still delivering your message, the better off you are.

If I told you that it was a really hot day outside, I am expressing this sentiment because—within the data bank of my brain—the feeling I have when I'm outside is categorized as hot. When I say those words to you, the data bank that is in your brain scans your historical perspective, and you register a feeling in line with what you have categorized as a hot day. If I live in a tropical area and you live in Alaska, I may communicate to you that it is a hot day, and you may hear what I'm saying to you, but the perspectives are so different that what I'm saying and what you're hearing are two completely different things.

In addition to the communication breakdown caused by perspective, there is often a communication breakdown created by a transmission problem. All of us have had the experience of talking on a cell phone, having a great conversation one minute, and the next minute hearing a speaker who sounds like Darth Vader speaking Lithuanian.

All of us send and receive communication in different ways. Each of us has a method or system whereby we excel in communicating, and we all have areas in which we are poor communicators. As you move toward your definition of success through Ultimate Productivity, you will be engaging a number of people in your mission. Your challenge will be to maximize communication and avoid miscommunications, partial communication, and false communication.

In the course of my business, I travel extensively each year. This puts me in and out of many hotels across the country and around the world. As a blind

> Just because you're talking and someone else is listening doesn't mean you are communicating. Communication is the process of successfully getting thoughts and ideas from your mind to someone else's.

person, this can be challenging since hotel rooms are set up differently, so in each city I have a new environment to learn.

Each time I return to my hotel room, I generally call the front desk to see if I have any messages. This usually works. But one time, while staying in a particular hotel, the operator answered my inquiry by letting me know that if I had any messages, the light on my phone would be blinking. I let her know that, as I am totally blind, their blinking light was not effective for me. After that she showed initiative, if not good judgment. From that point on, when I received phone messages, instead of activating the blinking light on my phone, she wrote the messages on slips of paper and had the bellman slide them under my door. Unfortunately, just as a totally blind person can't tell whether a light is blinking, he can't read message slips that have been slid under the door either.

This hotel employee went to a considerable amount of extra effort and energy to communicate with me and even elicited the services of a bellman to repeatedly run message slips up to my room, but in the final analysis, we weren't any closer to communicating than we had been before.

As dangerous as it is to not communicate, it can be even more dangerous to think you have communicated accurately, when in actuality the message has either not been received or was received in a manner different from what you intended.

The bigger your personal vision of success, the more people you will need to communicate with. When I wrote my book entitled *The Ultimate Gift*, the process was the same as the one I am utilizing now, as I dictate these words to the very talented Dorothy Thompson here in my office. The words somehow come from my brain, I speak them aloud to Dorothy, and she does her spelling and punctuation magic to create a book manuscript. This process involved two people.

But when *The Ultimate Gift* was turned into a movie, the process of telling the same story utilized the talents and efforts of hundreds of people. The more people who get

> As dangerous as it is to not communicate, it can be even more dangerous to *think* you have communicated accurately, when in actuality the message has either not been received or was received in a manner different from what you intended.

involved in a project, the more critical communication becomes.

When it's just Dorothy and me, there is one line of communication—one person receiving and only one source for confirming the communication; however, when you get as large as a movie production company, it necessitates that you create layers of communication. These layers are important—but they are also dangerous. Each time a message is sent and received and then passed on again, there exists the possibility of dilution and distortion.

Do you remember the game you used to play in school, where everyone is placed in a circle and a message is whispered into the ear of the first person, who, in turn, whispers that message to the second, then the third, and so on? It is amazing when a message has been sent, filtered, received, and resent by thirty people, how distorted and inaccurate it can become. The simple message "We rode in my father's Buick to visit my grandmother on summer vacation, and she took us to the zoo," thirty people removed, can turn into "My grandmother lives at the zoo, and my father drives for Buick on the NASCAR circuit."

This seems like an absurd example of a childhood game gone wrong, but have you ever handed your luggage to an airline employee and clearly told him you were going to Miami and then later had your luggage somehow make its way to Newark? Obviously, schoolchildren aren't the only ones who have communication challenges.

The more people who are involved with your team, the more potential you have. You have the potential for amazing productivity—or unbelievable chaos. So, as you are building your team to reach your personal success goal, maximizing motivation, communication, and implementation—with every team member—must always be on your mind.

Remember, a lot of people who think they are in management are actually in leadership. You can manage a project, you can manage a task, you can manage money, and you can manage resources, but you can only lead people. People must be motivated, they must send and receive communication, and then they are able to implement the mission that will result in reaching your definition of success. Great managers are those who can attract and retain great people. These leaders understand that everyone on the team is different, and you have to communicate with each of them in different ways.

Let's assume your family is preparing for the possibility of a bad storm. You may collect drinking water, flashlights, transistor radios, and all manner of helpful items, but once you get together all of the supplies and tools you need, you have to communicate with each member of the family where he or she is to go in case of a storm.

Your spouse may be forty-three years old, and communicating with him or her is as simple as saying, "If we have a bad storm, let's meet in the basement." Your message has been sent and received, and you have a high likelihood of success; however, if you try the same system of communication with four-year-old Amy, you may experience some pitfalls.

Amy may or may not understand exactly what a storm is or how she can tell if one is occurring. She may not be able to determine the difference between a serious storm and a spring rain. She may or may not remember, in a crisis situation, where the basement is, how she should get there, and how to unlatch and open the basement door. Furthermore, if more than twenty or thirty minutes have elapsed from the point at which you gave Amy your instructions until the storm, she may have forgotten your communications entirely. Amy may be further confused as she tries to differentiate your storm instructions from the fire instructions she received earlier, which were to get out of the house and meet at the lamppost on the corner. Without accurate, constant, and complete communication, Amy may be in peril because during a storm, she is standing on the street corner, or during a fire, she is hurrying toward the basement.

Lack of communication can be frustrating and inconvenient, but it can also be costly, dangerous, and devastating.

One of the greatest challenges among leaders who have the task of communicating the elements of a mission with a team striving for success is to determine how much of the big picture should be communicated.

For many years in the corporate world, the thinking has been that one should only tell people as much as they need to know to perform the immediate task before them. This is unproductive, if not completely dangerous.

Communication is the link between motivation and implementation. Often, people cannot be motivated or productively implement their mission if you don't communicate the big picture.

During my college years, I worked on a construction site as a laborer each summer. I was motivated to do a good job and wanted to prove to my coworkers, who were older, career construction workers, that as a part-time summer worker, I could carry my own weight.

During my first week on the job, the foreman took me to a pile of structural steel and showed me how to attach a crane hook to the steel. Then he pointed to a massive crane on the other side of a thirty-story building and told me that when the crane operator swung that tall boom over my way, I was to hook the cable to the steel so it could be lifted to the top of the building.

The foreman communicated effectively with me, utilizing several good communication techniques. He gave me my instructions verbally, he demonstrated how to perform the task himself, he observed me performing the task, he asked me to verbalize back to him what I was going to do, and he answered each of my questions.

So, confident that I fully understood my task and with the best intentions to perform it promptly and professionally, I stood by and waited for the crane to swing around my way. Several hours passed, and the crane remained engaged constantly lifting materials on the other side of the building. I continued to wait until it was quitting time, and I wasn't sure whether I should stay late or go home, so I continued to stand by, waiting as instructed, for the crane to swing my way. Finally, it got dark, and the crane shut down for the night, so I went home.

The next morning, I resumed my position next to the structural steel, waiting just as I had been told for the crane to swing into position. The waiting went on for a second day and a third.

Finally, on the morning of the fourth day, I was frustrated, confused, and angry. I confronted my foreman and asked, "Do you want me to work here or not?" I went on, "I've been waiting here day after day, trying to do what you told me, and I'm just wasting the company's time and money."

Then the foreman communicated the big picture. He told me that the crane costs many thousands of dollars each day to operate, and I cost virtually nothing in comparison to the crane; therefore, if I had to wait days or even weeks, it wasn't a problem. The only problem would be if the crane swung around my way and I wasn't ready to instantly attach the structural steel so it could be lifted to the top of the building. He went on to tell me that he needed someone trustworthy to be standing by at all times so that we didn't lose one minute of the crane's incredibly costly time.

As the foreman left me, still standing by, waiting for the crane, both my outlook on the mission and my personal definition of success related to the task at hand, totally changed. While he had originally communicated well and accurately the elements of my immediate task, his *limited* communication did not provide a bridge between motivation and implementation. Until I understood the big picture, the prolonged wait for the crane caused me to lose my motivation and potentially the effectiveness of my implementation.

Communication is not just conveying what to do or how to do it. It also includes when to do it, where to do it, who to do it with, and—the frequently missing element of Ultimate Productivity and success—why to do it. If you're going to tell your team what they need to know, they need to understand what success looks like, the total scope of the mission to get from here to there, and the importance of the part they play in it.

NOTES:

CHAPTER TWELVE

COMMUNICATIONS:
CUSTOMIZING YOUR MESSAGE

One of the most important pieces of information that you and I own is our name. All of us have had the mortifying experience of being in a professional or social setting when we were introduced to a very important person, and three minutes later, we honestly don't know his or her name. Obviously, we wanted to know that individual's name, and we recognize it is a critical element of courtesy and respect to call someone by his or her name; yet after just being told that person's name by a mutual friend or contact, we don't know it.

Communication only happens when information is reliably and correctly transferred. Obviously, in the case of our failed introduction, real communication did not take place.

Let's assume that you want to eliminate this problem so, at your next function, everyone is given a name tag. You might, therefore, assume you have permanently resolved the challenge of forgetting someone's name whom you just met.

Although you feel you have a foolproof solution in place, for me and millions of other blind or visually impaired people, as well as millions more who are not English readers, you still have not established an effective and reliable line of communication.

In my office building at the Narrative Television Network, we have offices on one floor and studios on the floor below. Adjacent to the studios, I have a private workout room. Several times each day, I leave the office and go downstairs. I stay in communication via a small two-way radio. My radio has twenty-two channels. While this is a very effective way to communicate, it only works if I'm on the right channel. If my office is sending on one channel but I'm receiving on another, there will be absolutely no communication.

No matter how motivated my team is to get in contact with me, or how much they want to implement our mission, the reality is that, by being one channel setting away, our quest for Ultimate Productivity is stagnated.

While our radios have twenty-two settings, human beings come with many more options than that. When we developed the Ultimate Productivity Profile for corporations, investors, and entrepreneurs to determine their own method to achieve Ultimate Productivity, we discovered that the widest variety of disconnects come in the field of communication.

Since communication is the most important element of creating success with the team you have around you, and since it is the bridge between motivation and implementation, we've all got to communicate.

All of us lead people and have other people who lead us. If you are an entrepreneur or the CEO of your organization, you may think you are the top dog, but in reality you have a number of people who are leading you. They are called customers. We all answer to someone.

You cannot become a leader because you declare yourself one or because you decide to be. You have to earn the title and the position of leader. Earning the right to be a leader first requires you to possess traits that others wish to emulate; but unless you can communicate and demonstrate those traits in a way that others can discern, you are not really a leader.

It is important to understand what your leaders or the marketplace is telling you just as it is critical that you pass along their messages and yours to those whom you lead.

It is impossible to be a great leader without being an excellent communicator. By definition, leaders are people that other people follow. You cannot become a leader because you declare yourself one or because you decide to be. You have to earn the title and the position of leader.

Earning the right to be a leader first requires you to possess traits that others wish to emulate; but unless you can communicate and demonstrate those traits in a way that others can discern, you are not really a leader.

Our business and personal lives are controlled more and more by the proliferation of technology. You have heard it said that necessity is the mother of invention. It seems to me, in business, that a new invention becomes the mother of necessity.

I have read many books written by and about political, business, and military leaders. In these books, many of their personal and professional letters are reprinted. It is obvious that before the advent of the telephone, everyone got along just fine. But once the telephone was invented, it became a necessity. It's hard to imagine functioning today without a telephone, fax machine, cell phone, and a computer connected to the Internet.

I heard a self-proclaimed business guru recently state that e-mail and instant messaging have revolutionized communications. They have certainly brought about many changes, but they're not all good ones. Because my e-mails are read to me, I may notice it more than others, but e-mails are sent so quickly, with very little context, that you're often left asking yourself the question, "What does he mean by that?"

Remember, if you're the leader within a certain circle of colleagues, your colleagues are very reluctant to blatantly tell you, "I don't know what you're talking about," or "I'm not sure you understand what I mean."

Effective communication requires interaction. An exchange, or dialogue, is needed to correct and fine-tune any potential miscommunication. The more avenues you have to communicate through and the more interaction you allow, the better the chances are that communications will, indeed, facilitate Ultimate Productivity by building a bridge from motivation to implementation.

Written communications are often prepared without expression or emphasis, such that irony, sarcasm, and the degree of intensity are not conveyed. You may understand what you're typing, but the person on the other end doesn't have a clue.

You could receive the same e-mail from two colleagues that said, "Wow. Yesterday I really had a great flight." One of your colleagues may mean that it was the best flight of his life, that the service was impeccable, that the flight and the landing were smooth, and that he reached the gate right on time. But your other colleague may be using sarcasm to express his feelings that the service was nonexistent, the flight and landing resembled a carnival ride, and the delay was measured by a calendar instead of a watch. Still, in the absence of vocal emphasis, you could get the impression that both friends felt the same about the flight. But if, instead of e-mailing you their thoughts, you spoke to them on the phone, or better yet, in person, you would likely determine quickly that one person had the best flight of his life and the other may have had the worst.

Just as there are methods of communication that lend themselves better to different types of interaction, there are people who need specific methods or multiple streams of communication. If your lawyer prepares a ninety-two-page contract and sends it to you for your signature with a Post-It note that says, "Read and sign," your lawyer has probably not communicated well—if at all—with you. His communication was not appropriate given the content of the contract. Neither did his communication avenue properly address your needs. A brief phone call or two-paragraph summary would make all the difference in the world.

To communicate skillfully and effectively, you must communicate in a manner that is appropriate to the message's content, using the best avenue for the receiver's needs and preferences.

As a blind person, I am not able to read this page as you are doing just this moment; however, thanks to recorded books and a high-speed tape player, I complete a full book virtually every day. As the author of more than a dozen books, as well as a nationally known speaker and television personality, people contact me regularly to share a book manuscript or screenplay with me.

Over the years, I have noticed that 90 percent of people, even knowing I am blind, simply forward me a printed document as they are seeking my help to get it published or made into a movie or TV show. Approximately 10 percent of people bother to have it recorded or even ask my staff or me what format would be convenient or preferred as a blind person. Given these two approaches, I will leave it to your imagination to determine which type of presentation gets my immediate and full attention.

Sometimes in a difficult or challenging communication environment, it means a great deal when you simply ask those with whom you are communicating if there is a better or preferred delivery method for your message.

I have the privilege of speaking from the platform to literally millions of people, and I have noticed that while my message doesn't dramatically change, the way the audience receives my message and, therefore, the methods I employ, shift dramatically.

I remember speaking to a group of research engineers. During a portion of my presentation designed to be particularly humorous, I noticed scattered laughter punctuated by the sound of pens frantically scribbling and notebook pages turning. These high-level academics and mathematicians aren't comfortable determining that content is valid unless they have written it down. They want to see it, read it, and hold it in their hands.

On the other hand, when I talk to a group of salespeople or media persons, they are distracted if not totally put off if my presentation is not delivered in a way that is totally verbal.

With one group, I am communicating with logic, reason, and facts. With another group, I am communicating the same message with humor, emotion, and visualization. Both methods are valid, but they are never interchangeable.

There are a few communications in your personal and professional life for which the best method is probably obvious. If someone is taking a phone message for you, it is probably best that he or she at least get the name and number in writing; however, a message that says, "Fred called concerned about his order. 555-2321," can mean a myriad of things that can only be clarified when the verbal exchange that took place when Fred called is communicated.

> The more elements of the big picture you can communicate to everyone on your team, the better your chances of success.

Fred may be concerned about his order because he is so excited to receive your product and service that he wants to be sure he can order more. On the other hand, Fred may have been violently yelling at your receptionist as he communicated his concern that if the order didn't get there by tomorrow, he was canceling.

If you don't know which environment you're getting ready to step into, you may be going into battle without any weapons. If you haven't already communicated with your receptionist that you want to be alerted to the different situations, you need to let her know that you expect and welcome her full understanding of the call.

Two executives might be returning from lunch and both receive messages from their spouses that read identically, "Just called to see what was going on." Executive A's spouse just had an extra moment between appointments and wanted to call and see how everything was going today. But Executive B's spouse is calling because Executive B was supposed to meet the spouse for lunch and is forty-five minutes late. This would be impossible to determine from a scribbled phone message but almost impossible to miss in a verbal exchange.

Written instructions, as well as verbal ones, always make sense to the person delivering them. Everything makes sense to me in my mind. My challenge in life is to get that message of clarity from my mind into a book, a newspaper column, a speech, or a movie.

As important as the routine, day-in, day-out communications are, it is even more critical that the motivation you feel inside of you is accurately communicated to your entire team. There is a big difference between what you want someone to do and what you want done, as I described earlier. Standing around waiting for a crane may be what you want someone to do, while having a responsible person on call to maximize the efficiency of a valuable asset (like a crane) is what you want done.

The more elements of the big picture you can communicate to everyone on your team, the better your chances of success.

No matter how much you are motivated, and how badly you wish to implement, unless you have accurate communications with everyone around you, you are simply all dressed up with nowhere to go.

NOTES:

CHAPTER THIRTEEN

THE IMPLEMENTATION ENIGMA

Implementation is one of the most misunderstood elements of Ultimate Productivity. Many who are not achieving their personal definitions of success believe that implementation means starting. As you and I have discovered, implementation is part of a seamless process that begins with defining your own success, establishing a mission, evaluating your passion, creating motivation, and communicating all of these elements in a way that will make success inevitable.

Many people feel, when they watch the 100-meter dash in the Olympics, that implementation means settling into the starting blocks and waiting for the starter's gun to sound. In reality, that 100-meter dash began for those Olympians years before with dreams, planning, training, qualifying, and, finally, the opportunity to have the entire process culminate in one ten-second dash.

Proper implementation does not come naturally to human beings. There are those among us who want to engage their fight-or-flight instinct and begin a lifelong quest as a knee-jerk reaction to some random stimulus. On the other hand, there are those poor souls who have fallen victim to analysis paralysis, and they are not going to leave their homes until all the lights are green.

> "A good plan violently executed today is better than a perfect plan next week."
> —General George Patton

General George Patton is among my favorite historical figures, because he certainly knew how to plan, prepare, handle logistics, and analyze all factors; but he also knew how to light the fuse and implement. General Patton said, "A good plan violently executed today is better than a perfect plan next week."

A great newspaperman in my hometown called me a number of years ago after reading my books. Complimenting me on my writing, he asked if I had ever written a column. I told him I had not even considered it, so he asked me to fax him four hundred to five hundred words. About ten to fifteen minutes later, I sent the fax and never thought any more about it.

For too many people, perfection becomes an unachievable ideal that creates an environment in which they simply never begin.

He ran the column the following week and called me and said the words that turned me into a newspaper, magazine, and online columnist around the world: "Just do that every week."

In the beginning, I would fret about each week's column until he gave me another piece of great advice: "This is a newspaper. We don't need it perfect. We need it Thursday." That was almost five hundred columns ago, and now, writing my weekly "Winners' Wisdom" column has become an automatic, routine part of my life.

There are millions of people around the world who have read my columns, and the first edition of them has been released as a book entitled *Today's the Day.* This all became possible when I understood the proper implementation principles relating to my definition of success as a weekly columnist.

Perfection is something we should strive for, and it should motivate us to move ahead. Unfortunately for too many people, perfection becomes an unachievable ideal that creates an environment in which they simply never begin.

As you and I discovered earlier, every time you take an airplane flight, you are off course the vast majority of the time, and the pilots would tell you that the conditions are never totally perfect. Yet, the reason we have an airline industry and the ability to travel anywhere in the world in hours instead of months is because pioneers dreamed of a system and created an industry that recognizes that, within the bounds of safety, there are any number of conditions that will allow for a perfectly routine flight, and we're all off course from time to time. The key to implementation is to take off and adjust.

We're all off course from time to time. The key to implementation is to take off and adjust.

Those who overcome the temptation to fall victim to analysis paralysis can often fall into the ready, fire, aim trap. This life you and I are living right now is not a practice game. It is our own Super Bowl, World Series, and Olympics, all rolled up into one powerful, passionate process. While we don't want to sit around contemplating the conditions and analyzing all elements until we lose the window of opportunity, we also don't want to minimize our potential by not going through the valid steps of Ultimate Productivity.

Anything worth the investment of our time, effort, and energy is worth planning and utilizing motivation and communication principles as we prepare to implement.

If you went to a local grocery store and noticed people at the checkout counter, you would discover that the majority of people who have more than one or two items came to the grocery store with a shopping list. They don't want to waste the time and energy it takes to do their grocery shopping by forgetting something they really need and then being forced to return to the store.

I remember as a child working on some carpentry project with my grandfather. He explained to me the wisdom of measuring twice and cutting once. His words have stayed with me for several decades. "If you don't have time to do it right, when are you going to have time to do it over?"

The old adage that you must plan your work and work your plan is really true. We all have limited time, energy, creativity, and resources. If you're going to reach your own destiny through your personal definition of success, you've got to utilize everything you've been given by employing Ultimate Productivity.

Rarely will you achieve more than you have planned, and you will never achieve all you can unless you have created your Ultimate Productivity blueprint. There are many ways to implement that take into account your and your team's individual characteristics, but all implementation styles have certain success principles in place that relate to Ultimate Productivity.

As I am dictating these words to you, I am seated in my company office. I already know that, while dictating this chapter, I will be interrupted by an occasional phone call or someone coming in the office with a quick question. This doesn't bother me, as I have never been a temperamental writer. But I do know authors who literally have to move into a mountain cabin and be surrounded with total silence before they can write. Some great writers get up early in the morning and write a few pages each day. Other writers start sometime after the world has gone to bed and write late into the night or until dawn. There are writers who use computers. Others still use manual typewriters. And I even know extremely successful authors who write longhand on a yellow pad.

All of these styles can and do succeed for writers who establish their own personal definition of success, create their own writing mission, pursue their work with a passion, generate their own motivation, communicate it to everyone around them, and—within a system that works for them—implement.

If you desire to be a published author but only want to work at your craft for a half hour every New Year's Eve, I submit to you that this will not work. If you're not willing to learn the most rudimentary elements of spelling, grammar, and punctuation, you don't have a chance. And, finally, if you don't learn the basics of the publishing industry and work within those broad expectations that have been established, you're probably never going to be the guest of honor at your own book signing. On the other hand, in most endeavors there are few rules that will confine you but many ways to implement your mission that will result in you reaching your personal definition of success.

When I started the Narrative Television Network, I realized that nothing exactly like NTN had ever been done before. Even though I knew we were going to be breaking some new ground, I also realized that there were certain basic rules and expectations within the broadcast/cable industry that needed to guide our implementation.

The industry utilizes certain electronic signals, band width, tape formats, and other technical specifications that must be adhered to. Television programs have to fall within standard one-hour or half-hour slots, and commercials need to conform to the style, timing, and expectations of the advertising industry; however, once you've covered the basics, you still have some freedom to implement outside of the box.

After we pulled together a little bit of programming and a few broadcast and cable affiliates across the country, I realized that if we were ever going to make any money, we would have to sell some advertising and fill up our commercial slots. So we turned to a book that listed the top one hundred advertisers in America. I felt these would be good prospects, because I have a theory on selling: If you're going to sell, sell to people who buy.

A lot of entrepreneurs and salespeople waste precious time and potential by repeatedly beating a dead horse. So, armed with my list of one hundred prospects, I began calling them all each day. I have had people sit in my audiences at conventions and arena events that later have challenged me by emphatically stating, "You can't call a hundred people every day." Well, I actually enjoy bursting their bubble when I tell them, "Yes, you can. It takes about six and a half hours. I know this because I did it for many months."

The reality is that when you cold call the heads of advertising at some of the largest corporations in the world, they won't all talk to you the first day, or the first week, or even the first month. You've got to be willing to break them in or, in my case, maybe wear them down.

So, day after day after day, I would call each of the hundred prospects I had established, placing a check mark by his or her name after the call. I remember well the day that one flustered advertising executive got on the phone with me and said, "Mr. Stovall, I don't know who you are, but do you realize that you have phoned my office fifty-seven days in a row?"

I chuckled and replied, "Yes sir. I'm well aware of that, because your name is right here in my notebook that lists my one hundred prospects that I call each day. And if you don't hear my story today, I'll be calling you tomorrow and the next day and the day after that."

Please understand: I am not an annoying, pushy salesperson. I am simply someone who established a personal goal, forged a mission, and generated passion and motivation that I communicated to my team and prospects as I implemented through my sales calls.

Now, you're probably thinking, *I wouldn't have done it that way.* I wouldn't blame you. Fact is, if I had it to do over again, I probably wouldn't do it that way again either; however, implementing in that fashion generated enough success for the Narrative Television Network to become a viable and growing television network. Had we implemented it another way, we still would have had to get our story and opportunity in front of the right people who would help us succeed through Ultimate Productivity.

You should never be married to methods, but you must be unwavering when it comes to your mission toward your personal success. Unfortunately, if you don't examine yourself thoroughly and honestly, you will find it very difficult to implement Ultimate Productivity on your way to success. We all have human weaknesses and, too often, take the course of least resistance.

Coach Wooden tells me that most players want to practice the elements of basketball in which they already excel. They prefer practicing the three-point shot or dunking the basketball, when in reality, free throws and defense are what win championships.

When you consider implementing Ultimate Productivity relating to your personal definition of success, you've got to know yourself and be willing to do the things that mediocre people won't do—which are the same exact things that you won't do unless you utilize Ultimate Productivity through motivation, communication, and implementation.

NOTES:

CHAPTER FOURTEEN

IMPLEMENTATION:
PULLING THE TRIGGER

No matter how well you have established your personal definition of success, crafted your mission, infused passion into your goal, and regardless of how motivated you are and how well you have communicated all of the elements of Ultimate Productivity, unless you implement, all is lost. More people fail to start than fail to succeed. There is no shame in striking out while offering your best efforts and being willing to get up to the plate again. The shame comes in never having tried.

Timid souls will tell you, "If you set a goal and pursue it with passion, you could fail and be disappointed." The boldest among us would say, "If you try and try again, you will eventually succeed. If you don't try, you will inevitably and absolutely fail."

As a platform speaker, I have the privilege of going to many wonderful events and meeting outstanding human beings. As I am dictating this chapter, I just returned from speaking at the tournament banquet for the PGA Championship where Tiger Woods won his thirteenth major championship and fourth PGA title. Tiger Woods may be the best-known example in his generation of someone who implements through Ultimate Productivity.

More people fail to start than fail to succeed. There is no shame in striking out while offering your best efforts and being willing to get up to the plate again.

He makes everything seem as if it is easy for him to implement. Yet I can assure you, the performance you see in major championships around the world is the result of many hours of preparation and planning.

One particular shot during the final round of the championship I attended required Woods to hit an exacting shot more than two hundred yards and stop the ball within a few feet on a very slick and sunbaked green. Most of the two hundred yards were over water. This strikes fear in most average golfers, but for Tiger Woods, implementing the shot is mere routine. He takes the same number of practice swings, approaches the ball in the same way, and executes the swing as he has done it thousands of times.

Success is never easy, and just because you have established your own definition of success and followed the steps of Ultimate Productivity through motivation, communication, and implementation, never assume it won't take a maximum effort from you. While the cost in time and energy required to succeed is high, I can assure you that the cost of failure is even higher.

It is important that you systematize the implementation of your success. You want to eliminate as many variables as possible and make productive implementation a part of your routine.

Speaking in front of an audience is recognized by most psychologists and those who study human thought to be among the most frightening and fearful of experiences. When people ask me how I speak to millions of people without seeming to be intimidated, the answer is quite simple: It has become routine. Any great performance, be it onstage, on the golf course, or in your pursuit of your personal goal through Ultimate Productivity, is a product of routine.

The human mind literally cannot tell the difference between reality and something vividly imagined. This is why you experience the physiological signs of fright while watching a horror movie. You know it's only a movie, but your respiration will still quicken, and your pulse will increase. But the more times you watch the same movie, the less of a physical reaction you will experience until, finally, it becomes so routine that you have no physical reaction at all.

If you are pursuing any worthwhile goal, it will be difficult. The difficulty is multiplied when you add to it the stress or pressure of pursuing something you are so passionate about. This can be eliminated when you systematize your implementation.

It is not as important what system you use as it is that you actually establish a system. Tiger Woods' routine works for him. But other successful golfers have routines of their own that work well for them. The details are not important; however, if Woods tries to use another golfer's pre-shot routine, it could throw off his rhythm and balance, and he may begin to think and evaluate instead of simply implementing.

People who work in high-stress, high-impact jobs, such as firefighters, police officers, and military personnel, are trained to react without thinking. If every time a firefighter was called upon to perform a rescue in a burning building, he stopped and considered all the danger involved for himself and everyone around him, he would be so stagnated in his thought process that he could not implement.

I recommend that you take the long-term goal you have turned into a mission and reduce it to daily activities. You simply have to determine what you would need to do today in order to reach your five-year or ten-year goal.

Life and success come down to implementing on a day-by-day basis. Make a list of the things that have to be done today if you're going to get one day closer to your personal definition of success. Then, as you look at the list of tasks that must be completed, there will generally be one or two you wish you didn't have to do. I suggest you do these first.

> Make a list of the things that have to be done today in order to get one step closer to your personal definition of success.

As the legendary coach John Wooden tells us, people want to practice the things they like and need to practice the things they don't. I suggest that when we are passionate and motivated, we should practice our defense and free throws so that at the end of the day, we can do the fun things, like shooting the three-point shots and dunking the basketball.

Most salespeople don't like cold calls, so they habitually dread these calls and put them off until late in the day. This creates a situation in which the negative emotion attached to the cold calls permeates all activities; therefore, if there are any interruptions at all, any unexpected obligations, the cold calls aren't even made, and the salesperson is one day farther from success.

Set the highest hurdles up *first*. Once you clear them, it's downhill for the rest of the day.

Any worthwhile goal requires the implementation of tasks we don't like. If it was fun and easy, everybody would do it, and they would all already be successful. Set the highest hurdles up *first*. Once you clear them, it's downhill for the rest of the day.

There are as many ways to implement a task as there are people. I am an early riser and enjoy doing my critical and strategic thinking between 4 and 5 a.m. I realize that, in your mind, perhaps, this puts me in the category of a minority—and possibly the category of *insanity*—but it has always worked well for me. On the other hand, I know people who do their best thinking and strategizing long after midnight. Some people must work in absolute silence, and others require blaring music. Some people like to complete one task and then go to the next in a linear fashion, while others like to trade off a few minutes of each activity throughout the day. And there are people who only feel competent and professional when they are formally dressed for success, while others prefer to work from home, in their bathrobes. It is important that you find your own power groove that works for you when you are implementing.

We all have coaches and mentors who lead us and guide us. They are important, but remember: Observe what they do and how they do it. What they do is universal. How they do it is personal and individual.

If you want to be a pitcher in the major leagues, it would be important for you to have coaches and mentors. Warren Spahn is recognized as having one of the greatest major-league careers of any pitcher who ever stood atop the mound. He later became a coach and helped many young ballplayers reach their potential. Spahn had great rhythm, timing, and a tremendous release when he threw the ball. He was also a left-handed pitcher. If you are right-handed, you can learn from Spahn's rhythm, timing, and release, but you should not start throwing the ball left-handed if you are naturally a right-handed person. You've got to use the universal principles that work for everyone, but implement them on a personal basis customized for you.

One of the things that concerns me about our school system today is the fact that everyone is expected to implement in the same way. There was actually a time in the not-too-distant past when all students in public schools being taught penmanship were required to write with their right hands. This seems absurd to us now, because we know that there are people who are naturally left-handed, and the thought of forcing them to implement in a less-productive way seems ridiculous. Although we have overcome that hurdle, there are still many examples of forced universal implementation in our educational system.

We all recognize those who succeed in life. They are generally creative, expansive, outgoing people who think and implement outside the box. They are known for coming up with new and better ways to do things. This makes them productive, and in our society, being productive—that is, implementing Ultimate Productivity—spells success. While we recognize this after the fact, rarely do we allow people to explore their own individual strengths while they are being educated and trained.

There are certain tasks that require everyone to perform the same way. Pilots and copilots have a standard routine as they go through the flight checklist. There is no room for creativity or individuality in the process; however, I am appalled when I see educators and trainers who think that all salespeople, writers, artists, and entrepreneurs should be cookie-cutter copies of one another.

There are more millionaires alive and succeeding in the world today than ever before. Despite the gloom and doom you may read in the media regarding economic conditions, the facts are that the rate of new millionaires is actually accelerating. The rich are, indeed, getting richer. People are succeeding faster than they ever did before.

You and I learned earlier that money does not equal success in and of itself, but it is probably the easiest way to

> You have the power to change your life, but first you must make a conscious and quality decision to find and utilize your unique strengths and talents on your way to your own personal success.

keep score and, therefore, compare and contrast the way to best implement your Ultimate Productivity.

Right after World War II, if you had surveyed average people on the street and asked them how most millionaires got to be millionaires, the majority would have told you that most wealthy people inherited their money. But that wasn't the case then and is even less the case today. Fully 90 percent of the nearly 10 million millionaires in the United States today are first generation. They earned, saved, and invested their way to becoming millionaires. While there are certain universal principles that all financially successful people have employed, there are as many ways to become a millionaire as there are millionaires.

You won't succeed because you're better than anyone else. You'll succeed because success has been defined by *you*, and there is no one more ready, willing, or able to fill your unique role than *you*.

As a blind person, I had a tremendous advantage in becoming a millionaire. It was readily apparent to me and anyone around me that I could not perform normal tasks in the standard way; therefore, I was forced to find alternative ways that best suited me in order to reach my goals. I was forced out of the mold that has been established for most of us to follow.

You are going to have to exercise your right to choose. You have the power to change your life, but first you must make a conscious and quality decision to find and utilize your unique strengths and talents as you implement Ultimate Productivity on your way to your own personal success.

While the whole world is trying to cram us all into a one-size-fits-all societal norm for success, the truth remains that your success is a personal destination known only to you. It can only be reached by undergoing the individualized mission for which you were designed.

Power and passion are the natural results of undertaking a mission toward your personal success. While the whole world may want to force us onto a crowded train leaving at a scheduled time toward a predetermined destination, the universe we live in is full of unique and magical wonders.

You have a personal destiny, a customized vehicle designed to get you from here to there, and more than enough fuel for the journey. If you will listen to and follow those who have been to their own unique mountaintops instead of trailing the herd onto the crowded train, you will live a life unknown and unimaginable to the masses of humanity.

You won't succeed because you're better than anyone else. You'll succeed because success is defined by you, and there is no one more ready, willing, or able to fill your unique role than you.

NOTES:

CHAPTER FIFTEEN

ACTION:
NOW OR NEVER

After interacting with hundreds of corporations and many thousands of people through my books, columns, and speeches, I have come to the conclusion that there is a basic disconnect between most people who say they have goals and their reality.

I have developed the Ultimate Productivity Profile (www.UltimateProductivity.com; your access code is 586404) to help corporations, entrepreneurs, and investors find the most productive path to their personal definition of success through motivation, communication, and implementation. I believe you have those tools in your possession now, or at least you have the capacity to develop your customized tools for Ultimate Productivity; but without action, it's all just a fairy tale. If you don't act upon the things you have learned in these pages, your current once-upon-a-time will not end up in your living happily ever after.

I hate being the one to have to tell you, but life is not fair. It is great, grand, and wonderful, but not fair. In this life, you won't always get what you want, need, earn, or deserve, but you will, indeed, get what you expect.

If you will keep your personal definition of success in the forefront of your mind as you move into your future by pursuing your mission with passion, your tomorrows will be different from your today.

Unfortunately, many people try to move into their future while dragging their past along with them. This simply doesn't work. Your past has defined who you are today. The action you take today will define who you will be in the future, unless you fail to release your past.

One of my favorite animals to study is the spider monkey, a small primate that shares many of the same characteristics as human beings. Spider monkeys live in the tallest trees in the rain forest of the Amazon basin in South America.

For many years, explorers tried to capture the spider monkeys. First, they tried catching them in giant nets suspended from the trees. But the spider monkeys were too small and too fast, so they could slip through and around the nets and scurry to safety. Next, the explorers tried capturing the monkeys by shooting them with dart guns containing tranquilizers. But there were too many leaves and branches between the explorers and the treetops where the spider monkeys dwell.

The explorers were frustrated in every attempt to capture the spider monkeys until one of the natives showed them the secret. And now, I'm going to share that secret with you.

You begin by finding a single peanut and placing it inside of a clear glass bottle. You have now constructed the perfect spider monkey trap. You then place the bottle containing the peanut at the base of a tree, and you leave the area.

While you're gone, the unsuspecting spider monkey will look way down the tree and see that lone peanut in the bottle. He will eventually climb down the tree and put his little hand right in the bottle and grab the peanut. His clenched fist, now holding the peanut, is too large to get out of the bottle, so—Presto! You have captured a spider monkey.

You can return an hour, a day, or even a week later, and that little spider monkey will still be standing there, holding on to that peanut inside the bottle that he really didn't want in the first place, and he can't eat anyway. You can place a whole bag of peanuts on the ground next to the spider monkey, but he'll continue to stand right there, clutching the one lone peanut that isn't doing him a bit of good. You can put bananas all around him on the ground, but he will continue to stand there holding that useless peanut.

He may eventually starve to death if you don't help him out of his self-imposed trap. You can even have other spider monkeys playing all around him, but the trapped spider monkey will stand there all alone clutching one worthless peanut—that is destroying his future.

You can take away his freedom, or you can take away his very life, but our little spider monkey will simply not be willing to let go of something of no value, even to gain everything in the world that matters to him.

After conducting exhaustive research myself into the behavior of spider monkeys—I probably shouldn't call it exhaustive research, but I have read two books on the subject—I have come to the inescapable conclusion that spider monkeys are stupid. But lest I be too critical of these poor little primates, and before you and I can laugh at their behavior, we need to ask ourselves one haunting question: *In my own life, what is it that I am holding on to that is keeping me from everything I've ever wanted?*

If you're going to have personal success, you have got to let go of all those images of past failures. If you're going to have peace, happiness, and joy, you have got to let go of resentment and experience forgiveness. And while you're forgiving people, don't forget the most important person you need to forgive. Please forgive yourself.

Remember, all of that garbage you're carrying around inside of you defines who you used to be—*in the past.* Your personal definition of success is a vision you can carry with you *into the future* as you pursue your mission with the passion that will lead you to your destiny.

You are a unique person with a special, customized, tailor-made destiny. You already have all of the tools necessary to get from here to there in the form of your own motivation, communication, and implementation. My greatest desire for you is that you see yourself in that way and take action. If not now, when? And if not you, who?

I am looking forward to your success, and once you capture the vision of your future that contains your personal definition of success, you'll never be the same again.

ABOUT THE AUTHOR

Jim Stovall has overcome blindness to become one of the world's most successful motivational and leadership experts, entrepreneurs, and authors. He is Co-Founder and President of the Emmy Award-winning Narrative Television Network, which makes movies and television accessible for the nation's 13 million blind and visually impaired people and their families. NTN reaches 35 million homes in the United States and is broadcast in 11 foreign countries as well as available world wide on the Internet (NarrativeTV.com). Jim is the author of several books including the 4 million best seller *The Ultimate Gift* which has been made into a feature length movie starring James Garner. He joined the ranks of Walt Disney, Orson Welles, and four United States Presidents when he was selected as one of the "Ten Outstanding Young Americans" by the U.S. Junior Chamber of Commerce. In 1997, the President's Committee on Equal Opportunity selected Jim Stovall as Entrepreneur of the Year. Jim Stovall can be reached at 918-627-1000.

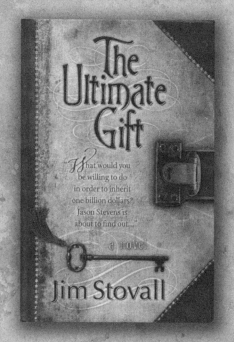